THE KINGDOM

OF SELF

By Earl Jabay

Logos International   **Plainfield, New Jersey**

Grateful acknowledgment is made for permission to use quotations from the following copyrighted publications:

Pierre D'Harcourt's *The Real Enemy* (New York: Scribners 1967)

Gert Behanna's "God Isn't Dead!" (phono record W-3179-LP) (Waco, Texas: Word Records, Inc.)

Norman Vincent Peale's "Communion Meditation" *(Church Herald,* August 14, 1970)

Case histories used are composites, the details of which have been altered sufficiently to insure the privacy of the persons involved.

Library of Congress Catalog Card Number: 73-89494
International Standard Book Number: 0-88270-068-5 (Hardcover)
0-88270-062-6 (Softcover)

To my true teachers—the hundreds of patients who taught me about the ways of the living God in their stay at the New Jersey Neuro-Psychiatric Institute.

Contents

THE KINGDOM

OF SELF

1

The Problem Is Myself

About twenty-five years ago, in a small Midwestern city, a group of young boys were playing baseball. It was a team try-out. Every boy was doing his best to impress the coach.

Robbie was a catcher. Younger than the two other boys who were trying out for that position, he was, however, a real beaver. Nothing was more important to him than getting on the team. There was no question about his talent. He was good. Any spectator could see that he was better than the other two catchers.

Late in the afternoon, the coach called Robbie over to him. Robbie studied the coach's eyes for some hint of acceptance. It was not there, but then, maybe the coach was hiding his feelings. The coach began talking about how much ability Robbie had and that he really gave a lot to the game. And then it came.

"Robbie, I hate to have to tell you this, but I can't use you."

It was like being hit on the head with a baseball bat.

"But . . . why?" Robbie fought to hold back his tears.

"Robbie—two things. You're not a team member. You never joined us. You play your game when you are out there. You are a good catcher—but a loner as a team member.

"The second thing is that you have a problem with me. You play my part, coaching the players and taking over. We can't have a ball club on that basis."

"But Coach!—I was only trying my best!"

Coach reflected. "There's more to it than that, Robbie."

"Forget it!" cried Robbie, as he stormed off the ball field. "I wouldn't be caught dead on your crummy team!"

When I met Robbie, he was a man in his late thirties who had recently been admitted to a mental hospital. Rob was severely suicidal.

"I've been struggling against taking my life ever since I was a young boy. Death has somehow always had a fascination for me." He was seated comfortably in my study, and I just let him talk.

"I remember that old Ford I had just before I graduated from high school. One night I took it out to the edge of town and ran a piece of tubing from the exhaust, through the window, and into the car. Then I started up the engine. Somehow, it gave me wild excitement to see how close I could come to taking my life. I chickened out, as you can see." He laughed hollowly.

"Another time, I tried to see how close I could come to the concrete abutment of an overpass. The car was doing about fifty-five when I hit it. Two days later, I woke up in a hospital with a broken back which still gives me trouble."

I thought of all the highway deaths and wondered how many of them were, in reality, suicides.

"This thing with death really frightens me." He paused and shook his head. "Well, it does and it doesn't. Right now, I really don't want to kill myself. But when I get excited or things go wrong, the first thing I do is think about some weird plan to kill myself. I have literally hundreds of ways all worked out in my mind. The idea has a hold on me. Many times, it's almost as if a dark, brooding presence comes over me and I have no power over it. I don't believe in the devil, but it's like an evil power—I find myself absolutely powerless to resist it. That's what brought me here. This time, I slashed my wrists. One part of me tells me I wanted to do it—another says I didn't."

Rob went on to tell me what he had tried to do about his problem.

"I spent years trying to figure out what kind of a nut I was to have these weird ideas. I became such a nervous wreck that I went to a psychiatrist for some tranquilizers. Thought maybe that would help." He sighed and leaned back in his chair.

"The doctor gave me some pills and suggested psychotherapy. I had already read a lot about it, so I began treatment. At the time, I claimed that it was doing a lot of good and that I was finally getting some answers. I think I had to say that to justify paying him all that money! After two years, I ran out of money—and patience. I came to know a lot about my past, but that old problem of suicide was more of a threat than ever.

"Next thing I did was go to a minister. Don't get me wrong. I'm not religious, but I heard that this minister was a counselor, so I went to him. True, he didn't say much about God, but he sure had a lot to say about his church. His congregation was very busy and active with all kinds of study groups and community-action programs, all of which I was invited to join. When I finally got to tell him about my problems, all I recall him saying was that I should make a decision not to kill myself, and that I should use more willpower. Oh yes, he said I should also pray. I was hoping he would pray with me, because I felt I really needed prayer, but he never suggested it. I quit going to see him."

3

I looked at Rob's face. Fatigue was written all over it. And despair. I felt pity for this man who had tried so hard to figure out why he was losing his battle against death. I sensed that Rob had a little more to say.

"The only conclusion I can come to is that my biggest problem is *myself*. I am my own worst enemy!—always have been. I'm a double person—maybe I'm schizoid, I don't know. I do and then I don't want to kill myself. I don't understand myself. I don't even *like* myself. Worst of all, I can't even *control* myself! For God's sake, Chaplain, tell me what's wrong with me!" he cried, putting his face in his hands. "Does any of this make any sense at all?"

I knew it was time to level with Rob.

"Okay," I said, keeping my voice low, "I'll give it to you straight: you are absolutely right when you say that you are your biggest problem. And the problem with you, Rob, is that you are a god-player. What I mean is this: you have tried to create your own little world with yourself placed squarely in the center of it. God has no place in your world because you have taken His place. Your whole life is a story of how you tried to set things up according to *your* will and plans. You wanted to be a king and build yourself a kingdom. The truth is that you are not a god, not even a king—you are a plain, ordinary human being who has never joined the human race."

Rob was listening now, not moving a muscle. I went on.

"That early episode on the ball field, in a sense, tells it all. Even then you tried to take over. You tried to take that ball club—coach and all—and make them serve you in the Kingdom of Robbie. You were a good ballplayer, but your enlarged ego moved you right out of the ball club. Even as you stormed off the field, you felt like a king. You told them you were too good for them."

I paused, catching my breath, but Rob remained speechless.

"Now, about this problem of suicide," I continued.

4

"Suicide is the ultimate act of god-playing—even though you never consciously intended it to be that. Look, when anyone attempts suicide, what does he do? He insists of having the world *his* way, and if he cannot have it *his* way, he will kill himself. The king in us would rather die than accept the world as it is. He has such a deep love for his kingship and such a strong faith in himself to bring it about, that any failure or weakness in himself must be punished with death."

Rob nodded. He didn't like what he was hearing, but he seemed to see it was the truth, and he wanted to hear more.

"The Kingdom of Self, understand, is in our heads. We spend years building this fantasy kingdom unto our own glory. The king's thinking becomes grandiose and his feelings ultimate. He believes all things can and must be done according to his will. And another thing; the king is never wrong. He is always right. Just ask him. He'll tell you. So when the castle really starts to fall down around his ears and the king has lost all control of the world in his mind, he will fly out of control unto his own destruction. Then the forces of self-hate and self-pity move in and become so strong that the king is powerless to withstand them. He does, therefore, what he does not want to do—he attempts to kill himself because he can't stand himself, defeated phony king that he is. It's not that he particularly wants to die; it's just that there doesn't seem to be any alternative with his kingdom in such terrible shape."

I glanced at my watch and realized I had only a few minutes before my next appointment.

"One more thing before you go: you are a god-playing king. So am I. Everyone is. You failed as a king. I, too. We are both failures—in fact, we even failed to fail successfully. But we are still alive, thank God, and there is much hope for both of us. If you want to, come back this afternoon, and we'll talk some more."

Rob did return. We will pick up his life in a later

2

His Majesty, the Baby

The first thing a baby does when he comes into the world is to establish his kingdom. He, of course, is the king. He is Number One. Because there is none higher than himself, he is in the position of a god.

Babies do all this their first day among us.

Shortly after birth, the baby is hungry. He is exhausted by a humiliating eviction from quarters which, quite frankly, he thoroughly enjoyed. Besides, his source of food is cut off. A complaint must be registered immediately.

The baby cries. He wants service.

A weary mother hears, understands, and responds, for nothing in all the world is more precious than her baby. The little fellow is introduced to the breast, and though he is not too happy with the considerable effort which is now required on his part, his stomach is soon satisfied.

But now our little friend has a new problem. There is an uncomfortable feeling around his buttocks, and because his skin is very tender, he again lets out a cry. Mother quickly responds. She changes the diaper, caresses her beautiful baby, and lovingly places him back in the bassinet.

Each time the king cries out, he is obeyed.

In a typical day, the king has about six feedings and three bowel movements. Roughly nine times each day, he tests the authority of his kingdom, and each time he is gratified with the results. All he has to do is cry, and someone will come running to attend his needs. Obviously, he is the center of the world. The world exists for him.

He is a god!

The days which follow are equally successful. A number of other people, besides mother, enter the baby's world. He soon senses and enjoys the love of one whom they call daddy. There are also those referred to as brothers and sisters who are marvelously sensitive to his every need. The world, beyond any doubt, is a lovely place. Not a single demand is made upon him. Apparently, he is the center of the world—a world which seems to exist for his sake.

As His Majesty, The Baby,* approaches his first birthday, he is aware that things are changing in certain ways. He can't quite put his finger on it, but it has to do with the attitude of his parents. Specifically, he is being restricted by such things as being placed in a playpen when it is not at all to his liking. And then there are such interesting objects as cigarette butts and lamps which are not only snatched out of his hands, but that action is followed by an angry rebuke. The good old days of unrestricted freedom are a thing of the past. The king has no doubts about the love of his mother, but her respect for his authority certainly leaves something to be desired. In fact, His Majesty wonders at times whether mother is becoming a rival authority.

*Sigmund Freud was the first to describe the infant in such terms.

Somewhere around The Baby's second birthday, a real problem arises. The problem is mother. She begins something called toilet-training. The king is *furious*. Not only is he not consulted about this embarrassing inconvenience (after all, what was wrong with the diaper?), but even worse, his earlier fears about his mother are confirmed. No question about it—she is presently an enemy!

This means war!

It is a war between two kingdoms, each authority wanting his own way. Mother may have more strength, but the king controls the bodily functions. What's more, he has one thing she hasn't reckoned with—strength of will. And a king that won't be beaten, can't be beaten.

Sometimes these toilet-training wars last for years.

Fortunately for civilization, however, this particular battle usually ends after a few weeks or months. But not the war. The beloved enemies are known, yes, and hated when they assert their authority. They are the parents, of all people! They are an alien authority which is continually imposing its will, its terms, and its power against the kingdom of the royal infant.

The egocentric life, of course, is not something a child inherits or learns by imitation. He learns to be self-centered by the necessity and very nature of coming small and undeveloped into the world. Babies are supposed to be egocentric kings and queens. By the wisdom of the Creator, a baby in this way copes with all the rigors and dangers of the maturational process. This helps us to understand very early in our discussion that our problem as human beings is not that we are intrinsically defective or damaged or malformed or evil. Babies are inherently none of these. They are simply mis-positioned—fortunately for them—while they are young, but, we hope, temporarily. Our position should change in the adult years. Our basic problem in the adult years is that we stand in the wrong place in our world long after there is any justification for it.

In that crucial period of time between toilet-training and First Grade, the basic strategies of dealing with authority are worked out in the life of the child. Many other things are also learned, to be sure, but none quite so fundamental as how to deal with mother and father. Their continuous and all too successful imposition of authority upon the child registers with him as an injustice and an outrageous indignity.

The Kingdom of Self, however, is not made out of straw. Every parent can testify to the unbelievable strength and persistence of a young child's will. The tragedy is, of course, that when a child wins the contest of wills, he loses. When the will of the child predominates, the result is a spoiled child.

I recall a situation in which a very small child was upsetting the entire family at mealtime by his spoiled behavior. The child persisted in throwing his food on the floor. Mother was kept busy mopping up spilled milk, father scolded the child, and the guests tried in vain to maintain a conversation. The child succeeded completely in capturing the attention of every person in the room.

What the father should have done was pick up the child and seclude him for a time without food or audience in a nearby room. It is absolutely crucial that the child does not win in its clashes with authority. The mother of John Wesley declared that the will of a child should be conquered by the time he is four years old. Susanna Wesley was a great success as a mother. Look at her family—among them John and Charles.

There are any number of times already in this preschool period when the will of the child prevails over a parent. Junior gets his way. He has power. Occasionally, the force of that power can bowl over a tired parent. The child soon learns that the bulldozer approach also works quite well when the parents are upset. True, brute force is limited in its effectiveness, but realize, too, that this is only one of a growing number of methods by which the young child copes with authority.

When small children cannot be powerful, they can be cunning and devious. The fine art of lying, as a means of outmaneuvering authority, is already in development at this stage. Nothing protects the king's ego as well as a lie, if it succeeds. Detection, of course, unfortunately brings down the full weight of the parent's authority.

It is amazing how sophisticated young royalty can become. Nowhere is this better seen than in the manner by which the child ingratiates himself with the authorities. The goody-goody, the overly compliant child, is an example of this strategy with authority. Nothing disarms the alien authority as quickly as a little cooperation and affection. If one can add to that an exhibition of growing talent and even an eagerness to please the authorities, so much the better. King Self soon learns the effectiveness of these disarming tactics. They build his egocentric regime.

In summary, the preschool period is used to learn the basic set of games people play with authority. These games will become more refined and more numerous, but none will be more basic or more widely used later than these archetypal games of early childhood.

The authority issue—we might call it the "god-problem"—is the core problem in human life. And it is almost insultingly simple. It seeks to answer the question, Who is Number One? The candidates are only two: God and those who represent Him, and self.

Our universal interest in this issue is more than academic. It is personal and vested. Most of the precious time in our lives, from the very beginning of life, is devoted to a resolution of this difficult yet fascinating problem.

Looking at later childhood—roughly between six and thirteen—we now see further interesting developments in the Kingdom of Self. This stage is marked by three characteristics:

1. *A great deal of time is spent using divide-and-*

conquer tactics on the authorities. This strategy in the life of the child is now developed to a fine art with the parents. The king/queen has noticed that at times it is possible to drive a wedge between father and mother. Being human, they do not always agree. Sometimes they openly oppose each other. One is usually more lenient than the other. These, our royalties have discovered, are perfect situations for getting *their* ways. When the parents are divided, it is possible to go through the breach. A marital war, extending over the years and finally culminating in a divorce, presents the child with a divide-and-conquer opportunity for which he does not even have to work! The parents do it for him.

The period of later childhood begins around the age of six with the introduction of new authorities called schoolteachers. A growing number of them present no problem, because they have long ago abdicated from all responsibility of functioning as an authority to the child. This sad situation has come about because the teacher himself is a god-player who now, in turn, encourages her pupils to become god-players. But if the teacher has not completely defaulted in the use of her authority, she is a legitimate target in the child's war on authority. Teacher is a new authority, true, but she is in the same category as mother and father.

Somewhere in the educative process, the child will try to turn these dual threats to his kingdom—parents and teachers—against each other. Here is an example of how this maneuver often works:

Johnny: I have a note from my teacher. (The note says that Johnny is not putting forth any effort to do his spelling. Even worse, the teacher has found Johnny stealing answers from the other children.)
Parent: You didn't cheat, did you, Johnny?!
Johnny: No! I wouldn't do a thing like that. But you know what? That teacher has it in for me. Ask the other kids. She's a crab! I never cheated.

Parent: All right. I believe you. But what about your spelling? She says you are not working.

Johnny: I try. (Tears.) I even ask questions. But that teacher—she doesn't know how to teach. Sometimes she even makes mistakes on the blackboard. Ask any of the kids. Besides, she goes too fast, and when we ask her to go slow, she tells us to see her after school. She should go slow in class.

Parent: These new teachers! I'm going to call the school board! How can a child learn anything this way?

The king won that battle effortlessly by simply turning one authority against the other and then taking the more egocentric of the two as his ally. The parent in this illustration is simply attending his own needs to keep, even at Johnny's expense, the affection of this child. "For, after all," reasons the parent, "doesn't a child need support and understanding?"

Not that kind. What Johnny really needed was a parent who would ally himself with the teacher for the sake of the child. This would mean conferring with the teacher. It would mean ascertaining the facts about Johnny's cheating and, if he did it, punishing him. It would mean telling Johnny that it is not his task to judge the qualifications of his teacher. It would mean encouraging Johnny to find some way in which he could put forth a new effort in spelling. It means letting King Johnny know that he cannot divide and conquer his authorities. Ultimately, it would mean that Johnny could no longer be king.

Real love, as Bill Milliken has phrased it, is tough love. This is not to cast stones at tender love, or to ignore the child's need for it. But in child-rearing, loving discipline is one of the highest forms of love.

2. *There is increased kicking against the limits set by parental and educational authorities.* Our little tyrants do more than test to see where the limits are located. Once the limits are discovered, an attempt is

made to exceed them. Every father and mother knows the frightening strength a child can marshal against parental authority. Even strong parents tire and are often bowled over. The struggle goes on and on.

The war on authority is a strange and terrifying thing to observe. Sometimes a child will carry it on in the home but present himself as a perfect gentleman and a scholar to his outside world—or vice versa. This holy crusade on behalf of the Kingdom of Self may also be waged in the streets and community, in which case the police will be elected as the authority to be countered. Indeed, as more and more parents and teachers default in the use of the authority vested in them, the police become the last defense against the tyranny of the self-deified. The permissiveness and violence-promoting nature of our culture is producing a frightening number of children who are defiant and openly hostile toward their authorities.

Not all young children, however, are defiant and hostile. A Lord who is merciful to all the rest of us has spared us from absolute chaos. God gives us other children who are submissive and sometimes even docile. I know. As a child, I was reasonably obedient and externally respectful of authority. But I know now that my "obedience" was really compliance. Most of my submission was to protect my image as a "good boy" who was beyond criticism. Ordinary human beings came under criticism from time to time. I saw no reason why I should be subjected to the unflattering judgments of others. Looking back, I now see that I always made sure my compliance made a generous contribution to my egoism.

Are there no instances in the early childhood period when a child relates to his authority with a healthy obedience? There are many, thank God. Is the child *always* opposing the authority of his parents and teachers? Of course not. Children work episodically. Sometimes they work furiously, even fanatically, building their egocentric worlds. But then, the episode of protest passes, quite often because of sheer fatigue, and the child again positions himself under an authority not his own. Watch him closely, and you will sometimes detect a sense of relief in the king as he leaves his troublesome, fantasy kingdom to again subject himself to the authority of his parents and teachers.

The security and peace which the child experiences under authority, however, is short-lived. The demands of being one's own king incessantly drive a person back to a conflict with any and all outside authority—parents, police, teachers, God. The child keeps on drifting back into this conflict which he can never win. If we ask him why he does this, the best he can answer is that he *must* do this in order to live. From his point of view, his *life* is at stake. He will die if he does not prevail.

Here we see clearly how very dear are the egocentric mental images we hold of ourselves. We would rather die than give up these dreams of being the ultimate authority.

3. *The period of later childhood is also marked by long-range planning and calculation.* I am thinking here largely of vocational planning, because the home and the school encourage a child to make up his mind as to his vocational future by the time he is fifteen years old. The expectation of parents and teachers is often that the child will not only decide what he wants to do but also that he will become president of something or other within his chosen field.

I have never done a study on the relationship between egoism and the selection of a vocation, but I am sure the two tie in closely. My own life is a case in point. My earliest recollection of "what I wanted to be when I grew up" was a military band leader. The fact that I knew nothing about music made no difference to me. I was, moreover, to be a leader of the band. Others could do the more ordinary things like playing clarinets and trombones.

Somewhere along the line, I switched from band

leading to the ministry as the goal of my life. There is a close connection. A minister is also a leader, and though I was unaware of my motivation at the time, I have since come to know that my choice of vocation was based much more on my egoism than on my pastoral abilities. No doubt a number who have endured my ministry would suggest that the only honest thing for me to do would be to demit from the clerical office. What has saved me from this just fate is the realization that a kind Lord uses even our sins and mistakes, turning them to our profit. The best we can all do, perhaps, is remain where we are and take on new and valid motivations for pursuing our careers.

Most of the egoistically oriented occupational plans are laid in the slow, long hours of waiting to grow up in the period of later childhood.

We are now ready to consider the adolescent period.

It is turbulent, both for the royal child and his authorities.

There is a diabolical way to make this stage peaceful for a child. Peace will prevail if the authorities default in the use of their authority. A pseudo-tranquillity will reign if the parents and teachers, out of their own egoistic needs, never say no, never counter, never set the limits for the child. A child treated in this manner will initially bless his permissive parents, but not for long. Disrespect will follow, and then contempt, to be followed in many cases by an attempt to hurt the parents as well as himself. There is a cruel justice which ordains that if the parents do not do their job, the child will rise up to destroy first the parents and then himself.

The normal teenage child comes into some painful and oftentimes shocking conflict with his authorities during this adolescent period. There are two reasons in particular for the storminess in this difficult period of life:

1. *As the young person stands on the threshold of*

physical maturity and independence from parental authority, he senses that it may at last be possible for him to be Number One. It is an intoxicating prospect. For many years, he has suffered under parental restraint, but now he is almost full grown. Fantastic physical changes have occurred in his body and mind. A whole new world presents unlimited possibilities for him and his contemporaries. His time has come.

The old, therefore, must pass away.

But the old refuses to stand aside; therefore it must be countered. The word "counter," however, is far too weak to use in this connection. The old must be *kicked* over. A new regime, comtemptuous of and disgusted with the old, is being established by our egoistic adolescent. He will soon be on his own. It is difficult to wait patiently for the day when he will live on *his* terms. And so, drunk on the fantasy of being his own god, the adolescent seizes what opportunities present themselves in this period to kick over the authority of his parents.

Eventually, the adolescent succeeds in breaking free from his parents, if not from being dependent on them, at least in being free from their supervision. The break is sometimes also a break from the family's traditions, social standing, and religious affiliation. The rebelling adolescent is so intoxicated on his delusions that the suffering he is inflicting upon his loved ones does not even register with him. The king is sensitive only to his own feelings. He is obedient to none but himself.

2. A second factor which makes the teenage period difficult is the anxiety of the young person over his capability to be on his own. He wants very much to be his own ruler, but questions whether he knows how to rule. The misgivings are well-founded. He deserves his anxiety. He has worked long and hard for it.

But there is no turning back. To be sure, there are a few timid souls who retreat to the safety of parental authority, make peace with it, and forever remain in captivity as children. Their number decreases, however, as the mood of our culture is increasingly rejective of authority. Most adolescents we see today are rebels—not in the sense that they are always in rebellion but that they periodically declare war on their authorities. The time to attack, of course, is when there is some hope of victory. Victory means my terms, my freedom to do as I wish. The periods of infancy and childhood were patiently endured only with the hope of eventually being on one's own. It surely makes no sense to turn back now.

But the anxiety regarding one's capability for independence is enough to make any young person think twice. Will I measure up? What if I should fail? Maybe I'm different from most people. Will these legs carry me? Have I got what it takes?

And finally it happens.

The king in the Kingdom of Self hands himself the keys to his kingdom.

Can he open the door of his life with them?

Of course he can, responds this young person in his earliest twenties. But these are drunken words. He is drunk on a delusion of his limitlessness and the fantasy of his omnipotence. He is intoxicated with the prospect of a freedom to do anything he wishes.

Let us turn to the period of early adulthood to see where all this leads.

3

The Kingdom of Self

In a person's twenties, the Kingdom of Self is, in most cases, fully erected and flourishing. Parents are no longer around to menace us. Our freedom to do as we please, however, is by no means unrestricted. If we work at a job, we have to be there at a certain time, work certain hours, and produce. If we are attending college or undertaking a graduate program, we are restricted by the demands of rigorous academic disciplines and tough-minded professors. As we leave school, we enter competitive business or the professional world. Everybody has either a boss or a fickle public or both—whom we must in some way satisfy. Add to all this a new spouse who, as nothing more than a partner in marriage, limits our freedom to go and come as we please. In spite of it all, a person in his twenties has considerable freedom from the restrictions of external authority. There are plenty of opportunities to test the power and authority of King Self.

As the self comes into the fullness of his physical

maturity, his goddish style of life is more openly disclosed. He becomes increasingly godlike, even though he vigorously denies any ambition to be a god. His "divine" characteristics are stolen and hidden. God has been stripped of His attributes. Man, as soon as he is born, declares war on God. The war is on this issue: Who is Number One? Is it I or is it Thou? *I think it is I.*

Out of that kind of thinking, a number of unstated and usually unrecognized convictions take deep root in our lives. Let us reflect on the following convictions of an adult King Self:

1. I am power
2. I am truth
3. I am right
4. I am above time
5. I am a messiah
6. I am the law
7. I am perfect

1. *I am power.*

After twenty years of cigarette smoking, I wanted to quit. Two simple reasons motivated me. It humiliated me to be pushed around by some dried-out leaves. In addition, if I contracted lung cancer, I would not be able to bear the thought that I had a hand in my own suicide by something as stupid as tobacco.

Wanting to quit, however, I could not. Thinking I had the willpower to stop, I kept drifting back to my addiction. I tried cigars, pipes, candy, resolutions, withering self-castigation—and even prayers, which always began, "Lord, help me." They slowed but did not stop my return to cigarettes.

Slowly it began to dawn on me that I could not help myself. Worse, the more I used my willpower, the more helpless I became. I was like a fish which has hit the bait of a trolling fisherman. The more the fish struggles, the deeper the hook is embedded. The only hope for a hooked fish is that the fisherman will remove the hook and return the fish to the water.

Some God-fearing friends who are wise in the ways of fish and people advised me to abandon my will-power approach. So I gave up. Surrendered. Waited. I waited for a power other than myself. I could never save myself from addiction. Salvation would mean being saved by Another.

In my acknowledgment of my powerlessness, Divine Power reached out to save me. I was strangely pulled to shore where One, a Fisher of Men, gently took the hook out of my mouth and then—unbelievably—made me free. And wiser. I know now I am not my own power.

My problem, I had always thought, was my *weakness*. It was a delusion. The problem was that I had assumed that I was vastly stronger than I was. The assumption of my own omnipotence had seldom been questioned.

The belief that I possess the strength to conquer the problems I create coincides with almost everything we read today—except the Bible. A colleague, a psycho-therapist, said to me, "You are a theologian. It would help me if you would define virtue. Once it was de-fined, I would try to motivate my patients to it." The assumption of this plan is that the motivated patient, once understanding what is right, has the power to do the right. But people do not possess this kind of power. Long ago Saint Paul discovered this fact and reported: "I do not do the good I want, but the evil I do not want is what I do." This painful realization caused Paul to cry out, "Who shall deliver me from the body of this death? I thank God through Jesus Christ our Lord!" (Rom. 7:19,24-25).

Our power-mindedness plays great havoc in our lives. Sometimes we almost kill ourselves trying to demonstrate our great power.

A certain woman wanted to rule her husband. This is something only God should attempt with husbands, but I suppose this wife felt she could do a better job than God. Anyway, when the husband would rebel, the wife would race into the kitchen, place a sharp knife on her wrist and scream, "I'll kill myself if you don't do it my way!"

This sick game had always succeeded until one day the husband failed to respond within the allotted time. The wife proceeded with this demonstration of her power and still bears the scars on her wrists as a silent testimony to the fact that those who play god must ever after look at the sad results of their work.

Egoists need to continually test their strength because they realize that they are not so godlike as they would like to believe. An acquaintance of mine told me how he had tested his power. He decided to lock himself in the trunk of his car. If he could somehow break out, this would prove that he had the strength to solve any of life's problems. Should he not be able to open the trunk, well, he was not so keen about living anyway.

Six hours after the trunk was locked, my friend crawled out by clawing his way through the back seat of the car. Emerging, he said, "Now I can handle anything!" And so we hear it again: "I am power."

2. *I am truth.*

Ever notice the tendency in our thinking to regard our present understandings as the truth? We regard the knowledge we have right now as a considerable improvement over what people had in the past. As for the knowledge of contemporaries, the fury of our arguments testifies to our conviction of our own infallibility. We need only listen to the conversations in the faculty room of any college or at the bar of the local tavern to establish both statements. Somehow, above the noise and din of the conversations, we hear each authority shouting, "I may not always be right, but I'm never wrong."

Look for a moment at the political world. When a corrupt politician is caught red-handed breaking the law, we seldom read in the newspapers that the politician realized his error and confessed his sin. Heavens! If he did that, the citizenry would probably forgive him and place him back in office! What usually happens is that the politician, even on his way to jail, protests his complete innocence and vows to appeal his case to a higher court. As the key locks our politician in his prison cell, he mutters, "The whole world is wrong. I alone have spoken the truth."

I once overheard the following conversation of two salesmen:

"You've got to understand your territory: what's true in New York City, for example, is not true for Grand Rapids."

"I don't understand."

"Well, when you're in New York, you use New York truth. That is, be cutthroat, aggressive, merciless. But Grand Rapids is a nice town, and you have to be like them. There, you use Grand Rapids truth. You act decently, watch your language, and look like a Republican."

"I see what you mean."

And suddenly this eavesdropper understood how deep is the human tendency for each person to manufacture his own brand of truth.

There are other examples of our insistent claim of speaking ultimate truth.

There is, for instance, a certain kind of person who has the golden mean as his goal in life. This individual, who is usually quite sophisticated, avoids the extremes on any issue. He is neither conservative nor liberal, but, he claims, the best of both. He is neither demanding nor overly permissive, but always fair. Some people are over-dependent, some independent, but our friend is inter-dependent. He is a man who does not see something as all evil, or all good, but as a combination of both. Behold, a man of truth has finally arrived to enlighten the minds of the pitiable extremists.

A clearer example of "the happy moderate" can be

seen in the case of the eclectic. An eclectic is a person who claims adherence to no position, choosing rather to take and use the best from all schools of thought. The eclectic feels this is a viewpoint superior to the distortion of narrow-minded people who unashamedly claim a biased position. The eclectic is above all that. He borrows from one school (they should feel honored!) for this kind of problem and from another school for that kind of problem.

This is the way in which the eclectic never needs to defend anything, because he has no position. With justification, others inform him that what he really lacks is the courage to take a stand, the humility to identify with others, and the honesty to work through to his own conclusions. In this way, he would avoid being a parasite, as well as pretending to be the source of ultimate truth.

3. *I am right.*

A few years ago, two men were eating dinner together in a restaurant in Newark, New Jersey. In the course of their conversation, one of them happened to use the word "perogative."

"You didn't pronounce that correctly," said his friend. "The word is 'prerogative'—not 'perogative.'"

This little lesson in pronunciation was not at all appreciated by the man who had used the word. He was obviously irritated by his friend's correction. "Look— I'm positive the word is 'perogative,' and stop trying to act like my English teacher."

"But you were wrong," continued the self-appointed English teacher.

What had been a pleasant conversation now turned into a vicious argument as to who knew the most about the English language. This verbal battle grew so hot and loud that the contestants attracted the attention of a waitress. The issue was heatedly presented to the waitress and to her we must credit a brilliant suggestion:

"Why don't you go next-door to the drugstore and

buy a fifty-cent dictionary? That ought to settle the argument."

The wisdom of this suggestion had instant appeal to both men. Mr. Prerogative volunteered to go. He quickly returned with a victorious smile written all over his face. "See? Just what I said. 'Prerogative!'"

"Here—let me see that dictionary!" commanded Mr. Perogative. "Just as I thought. This is one of those cheap little pulp editions. You can't trust them! I only go by Webster's unabridged edition. I'm sure it would support me!"

I have no word about this man's reaction after he consulted the Webster's unabridged edition. I suspect he rejected that edition also, because the desire to find the truth was entirely lacking in him. This man was fighting to preserve one of the deepest convictions a person can have about himself—*I am right!*

It is this kind of conviction that can keep a mental patient locked up for years in a hospital. This happened in the case of Tom, a splendid young man in his early twenties. Tom had tried for days to argue with me on the hate-filled issues of neo-Nazism, anti-Semitism, and white racism. Finally I turned to Tom and asked, "Which do you want—to be right on these issues or to get well so as to leave this hospital?"

Without a moment's hesitation, he answered, "Be right! I don't care if I never get out of this hospital!"

So Tom stayed on with us. Eventually, he was transferred to another hospital, but to my knowledge, Tom is still standing for what he thinks is *right* on the back ward of a mental hospital.

The stubbornness and rigidity that goes with this conviction of infallibility often takes a more subtle expression in the form of indecision. Many of us know the agony of being unable sometimes to make even simple decisions, such as what to order on a menu or which route to take on a trip. Major decisions, of course, may so completely frighten us that we become paralyzed. When this happens, we either get other people to make our decisions or allow the flow of events and circumstances to determine the course of our lives.

What causes this paralysis of the will? Why can't we, under God, make these decisions?

If my understanding is correct, the problem lies in our unconscious insistence that *I must never be wrong.* When a person makes a choice, he must run the danger of making the wrong choice and, therefore, of being in error. This is a completely unacceptable prospect to anyone committed to the glorification of his ego. Consequently, no decision is made, and the delusion of rightness is preserved.

Sometimes a helpful friend may try to point out to the egoist that by not choosing, he has already made a choice in favor of his status quo. This seldom dents the thinking of the infallible egoist, because he defends all past decisions as being the right ones anyway.

4. *I am above time.*

There are many illustrations in our lives which show us how our egoism seeks to raise us above time. Characteristically, an egoist lives mainly in the past and the future, which, when you come to think of it, is the habitation of the eternal God. The egoist evades an authentic entrance into the present moment, because that almost invariably results in a confrontation with reality. If there is one thing an egoist cannot bear, it's being forced to have a look at who he really is. The past he can review selectively, avoiding any unpleasant or unflattering recollections. The future is one beautiful fantasy in which, even if he does not always have the starring role, he always gets the best lines because he (not God) is writing the script. But the present time is what the egoist avoids like the plague, because in the present moment, he is inescapably disclosed as an impersonator of God.

But we egoists, nonetheless, learn to do certain self-serving things with time—particularly by our efforts to live above time.

Take a look at the habit of tardiness. I am not talking

about occasional tardiness. I have in mind a person who is habitually late. What is he saying by such action?

One of the things such a person is saying is that *his* time is more important than the time of others The tardy person has his own personal time schedule. Let no one interfere with his plans! Obviously, he is above the need to conform to the time by which others order their lives.

Our impatience also reveals our desire to live above time. A patient whom I was trying to hastily send on his way after a worship service rebuked my egoism when he said, "If the good Lord took so much time to make the world, why don't you have a few minutes to keep me going on it?" Impatience means: You must get on *my* time schedule.

On another occasion, I had listened for an hour to a person I had been regularly counseling. Upon leaving, she said, "You were very kind to listen, but you ought to know that each time we meet, you turn me off ten minutes before I leave. I sense that you are not really listening and that you are trying to get me out of your study to make room for the next person."

I was totally unaware that my egoism was showing. It seems to show so quickly in what we do with time. There is a strong tendency in us to use time, which we all hold in common, for ourselves. We keep on trying to be the master of it.

5. *I am a messiah.*

Few of us would have the courage to flatly say that we are messiahs, but we live it with shocking boldness. There is something about being a savior of others which deeply appeals to us. Messianic thinking was surely the basic fault of such world-conquerors as Caesar, Napoleon, and Hitler. Indeed, many politicians and heads of states are constantly working on this ego-istic impulse. Some preachers who have grown tired of Christ as their Messiah make an effort to establish little messianic kingdoms of their own. Social crusaders also get into the act. The world runs some risk of running out of the poor souls upon whose presence the very existence of all these messianic projects depends.

Some of the clearest examples of messianic thinking can be seen among scientists. Some of them were saying just a few short years ago that God was indeed dead. "Come to us with your problems. Give us enough time, money, and goodwill, and there is nothing in the world we can't solve."

And the world believed them and came with their problems, only somehow there was never enough time or money or goodwill. For every problem they solved, they seemed to create ten more that no one had quite foreseen. When a disillusioned world finally called them to an accounting, they bitterly replied, "Well, we're not God, are we?"

No, they are not God.

6. *I am the law.*

It is common today to hear people say, "As long as I feel something is right for me, then it is all right to do it." Such a person has unknowingly traded his human status for a delusion of divinity. It is every bit as serious to originate new, self-benefiting laws as to break old laws which happen not to suit us. The latter is obviously a slap in the face of the Deity who stands behind authorized legal authority, but when one originates his own legal code, tailor-made to fit his egoistic strivings, the results are just as disastrous.

Indisputable proof of our taking things into our own hands is seen in the homicidal-suicidal tendencies in each of us. I'm thinking of a woman whose death-wish for her husband is immediately stirred up the moment her husband steps on an airplane. She keeps fantasizing that the plane will crash, thereby fulfilling her homicidal wishes toward her husband. I think of a man, a solid citizen and pillar in his church, who, when he is frustrated, runs into his cellar, picks up a knife, and tries to decide which is the best way to slash his wrists. He has been trying for years to decide how to most efficiently carry out his violent intentions. There is something of both these people in all of us who try to be a law unto ourselves.

7. *I am perfect.*

I am perfect. Don't laugh. People—particularly we perfectionists—feel this way. There are certain times when the perfectionist *does* succeed with limited goals. The kitchen sink *is* perfectly clean; the typed letter has *no* mistakes; the books on the table are stacked neatly. In these small ways, we can claim a perfection which confirms the conviction of our divine status. And if this were the end of the matter, we might still be tolerated by our fellows; but what we do next makes us obnoxious to others. We take our perfectionistic standards and apply them to others. We expect others to come up to our level of performance. Failure to meet these standards incurs the judgment of the perfectionist. Talk about goddishness!

Now look again at this list of godlike assertions we have discussed:

1. I am power
2. I am truth
3. I am right
4. I am above time
5. I am a messiah
6. I am the law
7. I am perfect

These declarations from the egoist are almost always unspoken and usually below his level of awareness. Many of their sources are in the pre-verbal years where so much of the unfinished business of infantile self-centeredness is locked up. Others stem from idolatrous parents who not only refused to challenge young King Self, but encouraged him. What we see and hear in the adult egoist are the expressions, not the sources, of the problems.

One of the saddest and most painful expressions of adult egoism is loneliness The egoist often tends to isolate himself from his fellows. The reason for this is

31

simple. He can't stand people and they can't stand him.

The egoist may, eventually, therefore, recede from people. People cause him pain. They do not understand or help the egoist. The baffled king begins to suspect that people are against him. The weary warrior often chooses to leave the battlefield to live by and unto himself.

He calls that self-reliance. He also calls it independence.

Life in the center of one's world is the loneliest spot in the universe. It is a place which God alone should occupy, though God is never lonely. The persons of the Holy Trinity—Father, Son, and Holy Spirit—live in the deepest and most perfect communion with each other.

The egoist, however, displacing God and taking His place, thereby withdraws from people increasingly. He asks no favors of anyone, because he might be refused. He asks no questions because: (1) what he does not know is not worth knowing; and (2) someone might laugh at his question. He seldom expresses his opinion, because someone might criticize it, and that kind of pain is just too much to bear. Which is why, as Stanley Harris points out, some people like dogs far more than they like people. Dogs never criticize us. And it is a fact that egoists often care more about animals than they care about people.

All this hell—and that is the only word to describe it—because of this list of godlike assertions.

The problem with being god is that we have to be so busy. It is a staggering task to run the universe. We who have tried it have all but ruined ourselves in the attempt. We have finally come to an admission of failure. We could not do it.

Painful as it is to give up the delusion of divinity, we experience joy as we come to accept our humanness and are then able to say:

I am human—which means I end; I am limited.

I am human—which means I am able to accomplish

certain tasks within the lim
of my humanity but anytl
yond that is by the power of (

I am human— sometimes right and s
wrong.

I am human— a friend and subject of time, not ...
lord of it, not the slave of it.

I am human— sometimes helping others, but just
as often in need of others' help.

I am human— I live under law, for all authority is
from God.

I am human— sometimes succeeding in my tasks
and sometimes failing, but most importantly, accepting and using
whatever God brings into my life.

If you have seen yourself on any page of this book so far, praise God, because you are then beginning to see yourself *as He sees you.* This is good, even sometimes exciting, but also painful because "before him [God] no creature is hidden, but all are open and laid bare to the eyes of him with whom we have to do" (Heb. 4:13).

I want to suggest a prayer of confession to God, therefore, and invite you to join me:

Lord God, our Father, this picture of ourselves which You have given us deeply disturbs us. Our situation is worse than we had imagined. It goes far beyond breaking a few laws and making a few mistakes. We have sinned against You. We have attempted to rob You of Your glorious attributes and establish our false kingdoms.

We repent of our sins.

Have mercy upon us, O God.

Cast me not off, forsake me not, O God of my salvation!

Our faith and our hope is in You alone. You are all we have left!

Hear us, for we pray in Jesus' Name. Amen.

4

The Agonies of the Pseudo-God

The life of the pseudo-god is very hard and becomes more painful as his life continues. This is not because of God. The egoist's suffering is self-invited. It is earned agony.

This agony manifests itself in: (1) feelings in us—anger, fear, and guilt—which self-destruct; (2) an inner bondage so destructive that it can end our life; (3) despair.

1. *Feelings in us—anger, fear, and guilt—which self-destruct.*

The secret agent in the television show, "Mission Impossible," always receives his instructions on a tape recorder. After the tape is played, it automatically self-destructs by burning. Something like this happens in people, I suspect, when the hot emotions of anger, fear, and guilt are continuously fed into our systems. There is something about these emotions which seems to burn us up, particularly when the feelings are intense and uninterrupted. After a time, our capacity to handle even small amounts of these feelings is practically nil, and this results in a state of controllessness.* It is as though our emotional tapes have self-destructed. Indeed, these feelings can destroy the person.

Anger

I see anger as our primary destructive feeling. It finds many forms of expression. The more overt type of anger is seen in hostility, rage, sadism, temper tantrums, killing, and so on. But there are also concealed forms of anger: bereavement, teasing, testiness, suspicion, certain kinds of humor, and depression, which is suppressed anger. The most common and perhaps the most malignant form of anger is resentment. Resentment, allowed to fester, eventually hardens into a bitterness that is all-consuming. For a point to note about anger is that we store these feelings, sometimes for years. Some of our anger, it is true, is quickly discharged, but there is always a residue which is unconsciously stored. This is added to other considerable amounts of anger which never reached expression.

A friend told me of his anger as a child when a Griffin Shoe Polish truck backed over his bicycle. The driver of the truck promised to buy him a new bicycle but never did. My friend was resentful and vowed to get even someday. The day came eighteen years later when his wife bought some Griffin Shoe Polish for their baby's shoes. The father seized the bottle and threw it across the room, shouting, "Don't you ever let me catch you buying that polish again, do you hear?" We carefully store our anger, layer after hot layer of it. It takes only a small spark to later ignite it.

What is anger? From a spiritual point of view, anger is simply the expression of a person's condemning judgment. It is a feeling to which we do not really have

---

*My colleagues at the hospital, observing this process in certain people, speak sometimes of a "burned-out alcoholic" or a "burned-out schizophrenic." What I have in mind above may lead to this condition.

any right. Our condemning judgments are inappropriate both because we are self-appointed judges and because the true Judge's attitude toward us is one of forgiveness and acceptance. Anger, therefore, though completely understandable because it is such a human emotion, is nonetheless unjustified for at least four reasons:

a. It is playing God by usurping God's role as the judge of all men.

b. Since our judgment is almost invariably condemning, it denies the mercy and forgiveness God has extended to us.

c. Anger is an evasion of our own problems, because we feel very righteous, while the target of our anger is punishment-worthy.

d. Our anger destroys one whom God loves and cherishes.

Our condemning judgment of people is basically an argument with God over who is to do the judging. Paul understood this issue when he said:

My dear friends, do not seek revenge, but leave a place for divine retribution; for there is a text which reads, "Justice is mine, says the Lord, I will repay." (Rom. 12:19 NEB)

Well, now, if God is going to repay, what sense does it make for us to repay? James has the same thought:

He that speaks evil against a brother or judges his brother, speaks evil against the law and judges the law. But if you judge the law, you are not a doer of the law but a judge. There is one lawgiver and judge, he who is able to save and to destroy. But who are you that you judge your neighbor? (James 4:11-12)

One has no right, therefore, at his own option to judge another human being. The Scriptures are very clear in asserting that the tendency to condemn, which lies at the root of all our anger, is forbidden to us. Our

Lord said, "Judge not that you be not judged" (Matt. 7:1). And Paul adds:

Who are you to pass judgment on the servant of another? It is before his own master that he stands or falls. And he will be upheld, for the Master is able to make him stand. (Rom 14:4)

Then let us no more pass judgment on one another, but rather decide never to put a stumbling block or hindrance in the way of a brother. (Rom. 14:13)

Therefore do not pronounce judgment before the time, before the Lord comes, who will bring to light the things now hidden in darkness and will disclose the purposes of the heart. Then every man will receive his commendation from God. (I Cor. 4:5)

As we reflect on these quotations from the Bible forbidding judgment, we sense how they are on a collision course with our egoistic, judgment-loving selves, as well as with our secular culture which encourages us to express judgment without restraint.

Judgment seems so natural to the egoist in us. For most of our lives, we were honestly unaware of our tendency to judge. This is understandable, yet not excusable, when we consider that judgment in the form of anger was our earliest emotion. The newborn child's hunger pain is expressed in angry cries for food. It is no wonder, therefore, that we grow up feeling that anger (with its components of judgment and violence) is natural, even good. In the case of the baby, anger is needful, but there comes a time when we should "put away childish things" and grow up. We are to let go of judging, punishing (and sometimes executing!) others. These are the remnants of the egocentric world of childhood which are to be jettisoned as we leave the Kingdom of Self for the Kingdom of God.

Anger, then, is a person's condemning judgment—a

judgment which ignores the true Judge. The would-be judge is harsh and cruel. He adds to his condemning verdicts the violent penalties of punishment and, in some cases, execution (either in fantasy or in actuality). The self-appointed judge forgives people only when it is beneficial to the needs of his egoistic self-image.

The egoistic judge creates immense problems with his fellows because of his constant judging. The people who are judged resent and resist this judge. The egoist finds this very difficult to understand. Is he not pointing these things out for their own good? Should not he receive their gratitude for showing to them the truth? He is only trying to help. Unfortunately for the egoist, the people whose privilege it is to inhabit his world do not see it this way. The result is counter-judgment, conflict, and even war.

The egoist's judgment of others is only one part of his tragic problem. Perhaps the deeper tragedy is that he turns in judgment upon himself, thereby destroying himself. The results of self-judgment are illustrated in the life of Christine, a former mental patient.

Christine's problem was that she was continually setting up her own courtroom and then dragging herself into it. The verdict was always the same: guilty.

Being a devout, religious person, she would think something pious, such as, "I love God." This was invariably followed by a counter-statement: "But I love Satan more." And then would come her inevitable condemning judgment of herself: "Christine, now you deserve to spend eternity in hell!"

This poor woman reached a point of continual self-condemnation and self-rejection. She was able to tell me that after greeting me with, "Good morning. Nice to see you, Reverend Jabay," she would silently say, "I wish this (here she would insert a whole string of profanities and obscenities) would drop dead." Self-condemnation followed. At another time, she would ay, "I want to get well again," but then the counter-statement would come: "No, I want to spend the rest of my life in a mental hospital." Christine's verdict: "I am unspeakably evil to even think this way."

My ministry to Christine was simply to ask her if she had had enough of the pain and suffering which her judgment, anger, and resentment—all directed toward herself—had brought her. Was she ready for a new way which would bring her forgiveness and peace? Was she prepared to leave her self-constructed court-room and leave all judgment to God?

Yes, she was ready, I was assured. With that, I simply told her that I accepted her decision in our Lord's name and asked her if she was ready to tell God of her de-cision immediately in a spoken prayer. In a brief prayer, barely audible at times, but spoken from the heart, Christine set herself under the jurisdiction of the Judge. She surrendered her life to God and re-pented of her sins. I also prayed.

Our prayers were answered dramatically.* Christine was set free. She was a new person. She stopped judg-ing herself. For two days. And then she was worse.

The old feelings of self-judgment returned with a fury. Christine was in a panic as she told me that all was lost. It was no use going on, she said. Either she had failed, or God had failed—she did not know which —but she knew she had returned to her psychotic hell.

I countered her sharply by saying, "I'm sorry, Chris-tine, but two days ago a deal was made between you, God, and myself. We agreed that He is your sole judge. You also placed your life under His management. I

---

*My ministry to Christine involved more than is here discussed. This was an authentic case of demon possession, as Christine herself testified. Her tendency to condemn herself and others had provided Satan a wedge to enter her personality. It was necessary for her to first repent of her sins against God before dealing with the problem of demon possession. After hearing her moving prayer of repentance, I asked her if she wished to be free from the power of Satan and placed under the power of Jesus Christ. Her desire was very strong. I offered a prayer of exorcism, casting out the demonic presence in the name of Jesus Christ, and by the power of His blood.

don't care how you feel about that deal today, but the deal still holds. God has not backed out, nor have I. We hold you to the agreement we all made. Think about that. There is nothing more that I can say right now." I left Christine—but only for a day, which seemed to me like a week. When I returned, Christine was talking differently.

Since Christine left the hospital four years ago, I can report an improvement in her which is nothing less than miraculous. This is not to deny, however, that the road to recovery was difficult and painful in many places, but it was never so torturous as Christine's lonely world of self-judgment.

The position which asserts that self-judgment is not valid is nothing more than the follow-through of a Pauline insight. When the Corinthian Christians presumed to judge Paul's work as a missionary, he told them that their judgment mattered very little to him. In fact, he added, "I do not even judge myself. It is the Lord who judges me" (I Cor. 4:3-4).

As the right to judge and punish is taken from us, there is no ground on which to build our anger. It is no wonder, therefore, that the Scriptures are as severely opposed to human anger as they are to human judgment, for anger feeds on judgment.

First let us hear some of the scriptural insights.

Reflect on these passages:
Refrain from anger, and forsake wrath! Fret not yourself; it tends only to evil. (Ps. 37:8)

Good sense makes a man slow to anger, and it is his glory to overlook an offense. (Prov. 19:11)

Be not hasty in thy spirit to be angry; for anger resteth in the bosom of fools. (Eccles. 7:9 KJV)

Let every man be quick to hear, slow to speak, slow to anger, for the anger of men does not work the righteousness of God. (James 1:19-20)

And here are some words from the lips of our Lord which make all others sound timid:

> But I say to you that every one who is angry with his brother shall be liable to judgment; whoever insults his brother shall be liable to the council, and whoever says, "You fool!" shall be liable to the hell of fire. (Matt. 5:22)

In response to this last passage, a fellow pastor once shouted, "I can't accept that! Why, the only way I can get things done in my church is by getting angry. What would I do without my anger? Even Christ got angry. Look how He cleansed the temple!"

Yes, let us look at our Lord as He twice cleansed the temple of the money-changers. Bear in mind that (1) He was the Messiah, and (2) His action precipitated the crucifixion.

In the office of Messiah, our Lord has as much right to clean out the temple as a policeman has to clean out a gambling ring. Note, too, that the use of authority, though it may appear to be wrathful, can be administered without anger. It is possible for a father to spank his child without fuming in anger. Indeed, he should wait until his anger subsides before touching the child. I don't think Christ was having a temper tantrum when He was cleansing the temple. He was doing His work as Lord of that temple.

Whatever appearance of anger we see in Christ as He shouts, "Woe unto you, Scribes, Pharisees, hypocrites!" and as He cleanses the temple, is best understood as a calculated plan to provoke the authorities into eventually crucifying Him. Christ, not His tormentors, chose the moment of His death. The only possibility that the hardened hearts of Christ's enemies would be softened was for them to see the results of their commitment to anger and violence in a dead Christ. The basic motive of Christ was love, not hateful anger. The appearance of an angry Christ was staged for the purpose of saving men

If I understand the message of Jesus Christ, He came to free us from our anger rather than to encourage us to express it. Many of us are ready to listen to what He has to say, because anger is a major problem in most of us. We became hooked on it and have been humiliated by our anger. We wish to be free of this tyrant. If a person sincerely feels that his anger is no problem, God bless him. I wish I were at such a level of maturity. Some of us, myself included, are bone weary of our captivity. We are as addicted to anger as any alcoholic is to alcohol.

Perhaps anger is like alcohol. The social drinker sees it as "good" and does not wish to be deprived of it. Alcohol is no problem to him. But the recovering alcoholic sees alcohol as a poison to be utterly avoided. A little bit sends him back to his cups. That's the way it is with anger.

We who are hooked on anger and resentment seek a way to avoid them altogether, knowing that a little bit begins a volcanic explosion. To be sure, the explosions will come. Our freedom from bondage is partial. When we fall back into anger, we shall then have a special need of our own non-judgment and God's forgiveness, but nothing can take away this fact: God has led us into an unbelievably marvelous way of freedom from anger.

As far as I can discern, that "way" has at least three stages to it:

a. Immediately reach out to Jesus Christ to whom all power has been given in heaven and on earth. Anger is human power, and many times, demonic power. We need the superiority of divine power against such "power." In that split-second before impending anger explodes, we can look to the power of God in Jesus Christ to lead us not into temptation but to deliver us from evil.

b. Let go of judgment—let God judge. Place whomever or whatever provokes us to anger in God's courtroom. Meanwhile, we are to live, and let live.

God tolerates people even when they are wrong. So must we.

c. Decide (no matter how your feelings oppose you) on an act of love toward your "enemy" and then do it.

A few years ago, a deeply committed Christian friend of mine was witness to a fist fight which had broken out at his place of work. My friend—call him Fred—entered the struggle in an effort to stop the violence.

"Fists were flying all over the place. In the struggle, I was knocked out. I failed to regain consciousness, so I was sent to a hospital where I awoke a few days later. One of the fighters had knocked me down and kicked me in the head. This dislodged a silver plate which had been inserted into my skull during the war.

"My first reaction was one of anger. I could feel it building into a grudge. It was too much for me to handle. It was burning a hole in me. My pastor and I prayed for God to give me the power to love my attacker."

Later, I learned that Fred had sought out the man who had kicked him in the head, assuring him that there was no ill will toward him. The attacker, on hearing this, had the decency to weep

Fred's experience still makes a deep impression on me because he models in his life the way to handle anger. Our anger can drive us to self, in which case we will become judgmental and destructive. Or, our anger can drive us to God, by whose power we can become compassionate and forgiving. The temptation to become angry always gives us this choice.

Fear

Fear causes us to feel diminished, victimized, weak and helpless. It would seem to be the opposite of the feelings of power and superiority which anger engenders in us. But do not be deceived: fear and anger are twin brothers, the bastard sons of King Self.

That fear is the result of our egoism can easily be

shown when we understand the basic assumption of all fear. Our fears are based squarely on this curious assumption of omnipotence: *Everything depends on me.*

The fear some of us have in traveling by airplane can illustrate this problem. Betty M. is such a person. She called me in a panic to say, "I'm going to die. I must fly with my husband to California. I'm afraid to fly. The only way I can get on a plane is with four martinis—which I can no longer have because of my alcohol problem. What am I going to do?"

I knew Betty well enough to sense that what this highly educated socialite wanted was an explanation, preferably a brilliant one, of why she was so afraid. What I suggested in the way of advice must have seemed insulting: "Betty, I have a plan. As you walk toward the airplane, I want you to take your life into your hands, wrap it in a package, tie it securely, and then, just as you enter the plane, throw it into the air, saying, "Here, God. You worry about this!'"

I later received a postcard from California saying that she had taken my suggestion, and for the first time in her life had enjoyed flying. This woman who was so afraid of heights was even able to climb a mountain. At the summit, she reported having a marvelous spiritual experience of God's presence.

I am still amazed that by simply letting go of the assumption of omnipotence and trusting God, this woman had her emotional health returned to her. Betty's secret was that she understood that everything did *not* depend upon her. God was around. It was *her* problem, but *His* power solved it.

Betty's problem reminds me of a well-known politician who has a similar problem. He detests flying but is obliged to fly because of his work. On one of these flights, a new aide spoke to the panic-stricken politician and was sharply rebuked: "Leave me alone! Can't you see that I've got all I can do to keep this darned plane from crashing!"

The best thing the politician could have done was to turn the plane over to God and the pilot, letting them worry about the flight. Not everything, as we well know, depends on the politicians.

The various kinds of fears are innumerable. The fear of flying is only one of a vast number of neurotic fears. One could go on to mention the fear of death, failure, cancer, animals, water-travel, elevators, driving a car, darkness, germs, etc. One particular fear with which many people can identify is the fear of human authority in the form of policemen, employers, government officials, pastors, soldiers, nurses, doctors, judges, etc. Uniforms often scare us, even the postman's uniform. These are all authority surrogates, and it is easy to see why they are opposed so vehemently. These people remind me that I am not Number One. I am *only* an equal of others. This is bad news for my egoism, and so my natural tendency is to be both hostile and fearful of such authorities.

But why should one fear the authority vested in other people?

I suspect it is because we deeply believe that *power in any hands other than our own, will hurt us* (which hurt, we feel, is deserved because of our guilt). And so we fear power in others. Interestingly, we seldom have any misgivings about our own ability to hold and wisely use power. But watch out for others. When we have such an attitude, the world quickly becomes a very dangerous place in which to live.

Now, it is true that many times the world *is* a dangerous place. Even though most of our fears are neurotic, that is, all in our heads, there are many other instances where there is unquestionably a real danger threatening us. Is it possible in such situations to become fearless? Can faith in God dispel such fears?

There is no question how Jesus would answer these questions. He would say *yes*, reminding us of the great storm on the Sea of Galilee when His disciples feared they would perish. After rebuking the wind and calming the water. Jesus asked, "Why are you afraid? Have you no faith?" (Mark 4:40). The fearlessness Christ looks for in His disciples is obtainable but not attainable. We can receive it as a gift from God, but we cannot produce it ourselves.

Norman Vincent Peale, in a communion mediation, gave a dramatic illustration of fearlessness in a woman who was stopped one night by four men in an empty subway station in New York City. Her name was Phyllis, and

on one occasion she was staying in a hotel in the Times Square district. A college friend of hers had married a young minister and was living uptown in New York City. Phyllis invited this young woman to come down and have dinner with her and go to a show and have a snack afterward. So they did. Finally, they looked up at the restaurant clock, and it said two in the morning.

Phyllis said, "I'm afraid it's too late for you to go home on the subway. Take a taxi."

"Oh no," her friend said, "the subway stops right on my street, and it's only a step to my door. I'll be all right."

The two girls went down to the subway. There were only a few persons there at that hour of the night. They waited awhile, and the train came along and everybody got on board. And now there was nobody in the subway station except Phyllis, or so she thought. She proceeded toward the street exit when suddenly from behind the pillars came four punks with cigarettes dangling from their mouths and sneers on their faces. They lined up in front of her and barred her way.

One of them said, "You're out pretty late tonight, aren't you, baby?"

A second one said, "Would you like a little company tonight, sister?"

Her blood ran cold. She was at their mercy. Desperately she thought, "I'll run," but she knew that they could outrun her. She thought, "I'll scream," but she knew that no one could hear her. She thought, "I will fight them," but she knew that she was one helpless young woman against four strong toughs.

Then the power which had come into her life because she had surrendered her life to Christ manifested itself. And there went through her mind a passage of Scripture: "For the Lord God is a sun and shield. The Lord will give grace and glory. No good thing will be withheld from them that walk uprightly."

She had her message. It was to walk uprightly. She pulled herself to her full height, and started to walk toward the four toughs. They did not move. She continued to walk and approached them closely. Then out of the distance she seemed to hear a voice which she recognized as her own voice. "Let me pass, please, let me pass." The men on the outer ends turned and looked toward the boy in the center who was obviously the leader. He stared for a moment. Then he gave way, and she walked through them. As she did so, one of the toughs seemed to get the message, for he said, "That's it, walk tall, lady, walk tall."

She walked deliberately up the steps and then ran to her hotel and fell sobbing on her bed, but sobbing for joy. As she told of this to some of us afterwards she said, "I used to be a weak Christian. I couldn't meet the crises. But I gave my life to Christ. I surrendered to Him and He gave me the power."*

God not only frees us from our fear of people but even our fear of death, as eloquently illustrated in the life of E. Stanley Jones. At eighty-three years, Brother Stanley writes the following in his spiritual autobiography, *Song of Ascents:*

*The Church Herald, Aug. 14, 1970, p. 61.

"I'm afraid of nothing. What can death do to me? I've already died. You cannot defeat defeat. You cannot break brokenness. I've come back from my own funeral. I'm alive in the Alive."*

The conclusion is inescapable: the solution to all our problems of fear is a person—God. The solution is not an explanation, not a new insight, nor a new idea, but a Person. He is the very Person who solved our problem with anger.

And, as we shall now see, our problem with guilt.

Guilt

Guilt feelings in us self-destruct the person as nothing else can. Guilt is easily the major cause of all human breakdown. For such is the nature of guilt—it seeks to punish us for our wrongdoing.

Before we talk about our guilt feelings, I want to say a word about the actuality of our legal guilt before the Judge of all the earth.

So that we may think more clearly, let us understand, following the guidance of Romans 1 and 2, that God finds us guilty of (1) displacing Him and (2) breaking His moral code. Guilt as a result of commandment-breaking is easily understood, but we are far less willing to perceive the cause of our commandment breaking: God-displacement. It is this latter action which is the sin from which all other sins flow. When God is displaced, He is replaced with the egoist himself as god. He is a phony god—made such by simply standing in the place of Deity. This is the basic sin of which every person is guilty.

This double cause of guilt can be illustrated by marital unfaithfulness. When a man, let us say, has an affair with another woman, the complaint of the man's wife is not that her husband has violated the Seventh Commandment, but that he has jilted *her*. He has preferred another woman to *her*, and this is what really

---

*E. Stanley Jones, A Song of Ascents, (New York: Abingdon). 1968, P. 140

hurts. The wife is probably willing to forgive the legal violation of their marriage if only her husband will again choose *her* and reject the paramour. The root problem is the displacement of persons.

Do people feel guilty for displacing God? Perhaps there is only a fleeting awareness in the case of the egocentric who is all wrapped up in himself, but when once one comes into contact with the living God and *then* rejects Him, there most certainly is guilt. The closer one has come to God in all His holiness, the greater the guilt he feels.

I have just finished counseling a lesbian. She claims to be a liberated person. "Long ago I liberated myself from all conventional morality. Besides, everyone is bisexual, so what difference does it make whether I go to bed with a man or a woman?"

"I'm puzzled," I responded, ignoring her question, "as to why you asked to see me."

"Well, it's that I *do* feel guilty about being a lesbian, even though I should not. There's no reason to feel ashamed, and yet I am. Why do I feel this way?"

I tried to explain, without much success, that she knew very well that she was breaking God's laws with her sexual conduct. "I know you feel guilty. You are *supposed* to feel guilty when you break the commandments of God."

And what is true of this woman, is true for us all. Our guilty consciences relentlessly testify that we have broken God's laws.

Another major source of guilt comes from the impossible, perfectionistic standards which we godplayers establish as our own private code of ethics. This explains why a very moral, externally religious person can have a nervous breakdown caused by nothing else than guilt. This is the kind of guilt that is produced when one sets for himself impossible expectations.

I'm thinking right now of a thirty-year-old woman who came to me for help with her problems. She was deeply committed to the church and spoke freely of her love for God and the sanctified life. I am sure she spoke the truth. She was a marvelous Christian externally, but inwardly there was no place in her thinking for God, as was proven by the cruel perfectionistic standards she set for herself. Here are just a few of the things she daily expected of herself:

a. "I feel I should always be one step ahead of my husband. I'm first into bed at night and first out of bed in the morning. It's a kind of game we play, and I never let him win."

b. A near complete domination of the living habits of her family. They could use only certain rooms and sit only in certain chairs.

c. Her husband's ashtrays were emptied hourly. She spent the time in-between despising his "dirty habit."

d. All dirty clothing had to be washed at night. Woolen clothes had to be pressed after each wearing.

e. "I can't say no to people. At my church, for example, I just keep getting more and more to do. I spend half my time doing church work. I'd like to say no, but I can't. They [sic] won't let me."

f. Colors in her world had to match. It made her nervous when colors clashed; it would take her days to select clothing and weeks to buy furniture.

This poor woman had set all these standards *herself*. No one told her to do these things—no man and certainly not God. I do not agree with my psychologist colleague, with whom I conferred on this case, that the basic problem was an overly strict mother who had mishandled the toilet-training of her daughter. Such an explanation would, it seems to me, deepen the woman's problem by shifting responsibility from herself and judging a key authority person in her life rather than coming to terms with that person. I do not deny that, in some unconscious way, mother's influence affects each of us, but the point I am making here is that we use *whatever* we have learned, be it good or bad, in the service of our egoism. In the present instance, our pious woman made her own "laws," using, I am sure, the materials of her childhood training. These "laws" demanded more and still more. Finally, even a strong person such as this religious person was, would break under the strain.

True, not all people suffer from their perfectionism as this woman did. I am thinking of the people who have defective consciences, commonly called sociopaths. Somehow in the process of growing up, they ruined the delicate machinery of their God-given consciences. Since the conscience no longer functions, and because the sociopath's mind gets some sort of perverted pleasure out of living above the law and outsmarting authority, feelings of guilt seldom register with him. There is something of this in every person, but, since most of us are blessed with consciences which work all too well, guilt is a major and painful problem to us. Guilt, you recall, self-destructs a person. Guilt guns us down (from the inside).

What can we do to remove these guilt feelings? God has given us a straight answer to that question.

The answer is: Do nothing.

The Divine counsel is for us to abandon all our determined efforts at self-atonement. This means, for example, the end of this nonsense about catharsis from guilt achieved merely by speaking of our guilt feelings. What God has in mind is for us to *wait to be saved* from our guilt by His devices. What has happened is that our guilt has swept us out into the treacherous offshore currents of our lives, and we can't get back. The situation is beyond us. As the ocean currents are too strong to overcome, so our guilt, because of its historical unchangeableness, is impossible to change.

Each summer, a number of swimmers are swept into the strong ocean currents off the New Jersey shore. The first impulse of the victim is to make a mighty effort to swim to shore. This is not possible when the currents are really strong. If another swimmer attempts a rescue, he, too, will get swept out and will likely be pulled down by the panicked victim. The best thing he can do is wait—just wait for the lifeguard to swim out with a buoy on a rope. So with guilt.

But what is the *solution* to the guilt problem?

The solution, it must be clearly seen, is not a set of ideas, nor an insight, nor even new feelings and attitudes. *The solution is a Person.* We await a Person to save us from our guilt.

God sent that Person in Jesus Christ. God has already dealt decisively with our guilt through the person and work of Jesus Christ. The great drama of our forgiveness has all been worked out historically in Jesus Christ, the Lamb of God who made full and perfect atonement for our sin and guilt. What this means is that God has forgiven us. He is reconciled to us:

> God was in Christ reconciling the world to himself, not counting their trespasses against them, and entrusting to us the message of reconciliation. (II Cor. 5:19)

God has pardoned us! There is nothing to do except receive that *Person* into our lives.

Perhaps you thought I was going to say, There is nothing to do except receive that *pardon.* But God did not enter human history merely to ease our guilt feelings. He came to establish His Kingdom—*in* us. Therefore, the Person first and then the pardon. One does not receive the pardon until he has made a place in his life for the presence of that Person, Jesus Christ.

This Person's entrance into our lives, however, is a problem to us. If we invite Him into our lives, He must come as God because He *is* God. He cannot deny what He is. That means that I must resign as god—if I want the forgiveness and pardon—because it is impossible to have two Gods around; one of us has to go. It is impossible for God to be in my life, and I still be Number One. This is every man's dilemma.

So the answer to our guilt problem is a Person. Earlier we saw that the solution to the problem of anger and fear was God. He is the solution also to guilt. When God in Jesus Christ is invited to establish the Kingdom of God in us, we will not only receive forgiveness from every sin and all guilt, but experience that forgiveness as well.

2. The Bondage of the Self to the Self.

You and I were fashioned by the Creator to serve Him as Lord. When we, like Adam and Eve, send the Lord God out of the garden of our lives, the lordship of our lives falls into our own hands.

The self now serves himself as lord. In so doing, we live unnaturally toward ourselves, for the self must now attempt to control the self. In this diabolic, tragic way, the self makes himself a prisoner of himself.

This is why we complain, "I am my own worst enemy," and "I hate myself," and "I do not feel free to do what I should do," and "*I* am my biggest problem."

The self is in bondage to the self—rather than to the Lord God.

The nature of our bondage to self is of a particular kind. Bondage is our inability to begin when we wish to begin, and cease when we wish to cease. Think of a toboggan. The toboggan is on the top of a hill, and six people are seated on it. They are ready to go. They *want* to go, but the toboggan is in wet snow and cannot move with all the weight on it. The toboggan, we may say, is in bondage. It cannot begin, though everyone wants to begin the ride.

Someone now gives the toboggan a push. It is free— out of bondage. But now there is a new kind of problem. We want to stop it from heading for a tree, let us say. But there are no brakes or steering apparatus on a toboggan, and so, wanting to stop and unable to, we are again in bondage. Freedom, in this illustration, would mean the ability to stop the toboggan.

People are very much like toboggans in that it is difficult for us to stop once we begin. A little resentment nursed along, a little flirtation with another man's wife, a little drink each day at the cocktail hour —and we are off to the races. We get carried along and eventually find that things are out of our control. Wanting to stop, we cannot. We are in bondage.

Eventually, the pain of our bondage becomes so intense that we say we want to do something about our problem. We want to make friends with the person we resent, begin to live normally with our own wife, and do something about our alcohol problem. We want to begin—but can't. Our accelerator does not work. We are in bondage.

This is why all of us can identify with the apostle Paul before his conversion when he says:

> I can will what is right, but I cannot do it. For I do not do the good I want, but the evil I do not want is what I do. (Rom. 7:18-19)

Paul was in the bondage of religious perfectionism. He wanted to keep the Jewish law—perfectly. That was his bondage, and it drove him to a point of despair. But religious perfectionism may not be your particular bondage, so let me list a few of the ways in which we modern people express our bondage. It may be of help to classify some of our bondages:

The Bondage of Authority-Hatred: persistent resentments, a state of unreconciliation, continual jealousy, argumentativeness, habitual procrastination, suspiciousness, rebellion, defamation of the character and office of those in authority, continual fear of authority, recurrent religious doubts, arguments with God, atheism, chronic laziness, inaction, living above the laws of God and man, adamant unteachableness, continual parent-child conflict, chronic complaining, etc.

The Bondage of People-Hatred on the Peer Level:

persistent resentments, grudges, a state of unrecon ciliation, lust for power, argumentativeness, jealousy, suspicion, inability to be equal with people because we feel over or under them, fear of closeness, tardiness, continual marital conflict, unresolved grief over the loss of loved ones, racial prejudice and discrimination, one-up-manship, chronic complaining, etc.

The Bondage of an Overpowering Attraction to Violence: stealing, homicide, suicide, rape, continual fascination with violence on TV, uncontrollable bursts of hot temper, compulsion to take needless chances in sports or driving cars, preoccupation with guns and knives, etc.

The Bondage of the Body: constant worry about one's health, insomnia, nervous tics (coughing, muscular spasms, scratching, biting), chronic physical illness, allergies, accident proneness, etc.

The Bondage of Sex: repeated adultery, promiscuity, compulsion to rape, compulsive masturbation, sexual perversions, homosexuality, continual preoccupation with pornography, frigidity, impotence, etc.

The Bondage of the Mind: recurrent moods of depression, obsessive bizarre fantasies, persistent weird ideas and delusions, perfectionistic strivings, constant worry, insomnia, obsession with one's inferiority feelings, compulsive TV viewing, compulsive reading, compulsive counting, endless indecision, never-ending schemes of grandiosity, adamant unteachableness, persistent anxiety, paralyzing fear, fear of disaster, persistent need to run from problems, relentless feelings of guilt, bottomless anger, snobbishness, etc.

The Bondage of Ideologies: hooked on being a protester no matter what the issue, hooked on a system of fixed ideas (Communism, religious liberalism, religious fundamentalism, Freudianism, etc. , etc.), fanaticism (religious, sports, psychiatric, hippyism, etc.), etc.

The Bondage of Things: over-indulgence in food, money-madness, gambling, stealing, persistent greed and unending lists of gadgets for our comfort and ease, continual coveting, security-madness, chronic discontent, compulsive purchasing (clothes, cars, furniture, homes, etc.), etc.

The Bondage of Chemicals: alcohol, tobacco, heroin, LSD, numerous drugs (tranquilizers, mood-elevators, aspirin, pep pills), etc.

The Bondage of Words: compulsive use of profanity, obscenity, repetitious religious rituals, meaningless prayers, inability to resist telling a lie, broken-record chatterbox talking, temper tantrums, inability to speak up, over-talking, silence, etc.

The Bondage of Time: habitual tardiness, always talking about the good old days, fear of growing old, impatience, disregard for time, appointment-breaking, compulsive clock-watching, inability to wait, worry, fear of the future, etc.

Take your pick. It is tempting to assign bondages to those blind souls who inhabit the world with us; it is ego-slaying to select our own. Our diagnosis of others' bondages may be both accurate and brilliant, but diagnosis is a waste of time until the person himself not only admits but accepts the reality of his bondage.

Several of my colleagues have found this to be true even in the case of schizophrenia.* They challenge the current practice of shielding the patient from the diagnosis, pointing not only to the benefits for the patient of openness, but also to the patient's desire to know the truth. It is doubtful whether a person with schizophrenia can really begin to deal with his illness until he is able to say, "I am a schizophrenic." Until this frank admission is made, any help offered such a person will only be understood as good advice for other people who have such a problem.

---

*Miriam Siegler, Frances E. Cheek, and Humphry Osmond, "Attitudes toward Naming the Illness," *Mental Hygiene,* 52 (1968) :2.

People in Alcoholics Anonymous are especially aware of the need to make a flat statement with regard to their bondage. Each speaker at their open meetings begins his witness by saying, "My name is _____, and I am an alcoholic." This may seem like a very simple and obvious thing to say, but not so. It is agony to speak those words. They have a way of sticking in our throats because they play havoc with our egoism. This simple, honest admission—"I am an alcoholic"—is usually preceded by years of hedging and dishonesty with regard to the bondage. For years, the alcoholic said, "I am *not* an alcoholic," or, "I am a little bit alcoholic," or "Maybe I am." Not until he is able to both admit and accept that he is an alcoholic, will a person truly want to do anything about his problem.

If it is true that we are *all* in bondage similar to alcoholism, it is time we become honest with ourselves and lay claim to what we have. Again, make your selection of the more than 100 bondages listed above. Remember that the bondage is yours only when *you* say it belongs to you. The judgment of others with regard to the bondages we are under may be deadly accurate, and surely we should listen to these people, but the crucial matter is not the diagnosis of others but what you can now accept as your bondage.

When my daughter, on one occasion, said to me, "Dad, you are a crab!" my immediate reaction was to deny the unpleasant charge. Upon a few centuries of reflection, however, I had to admit that she was right and accept the bondage. I am a crab.

I have since come to understand that not only am I a crab, but I will *always* be one. As the alcoholic can never be cured of his alcoholism, so I will never be cured of my crabbiness. There are no cures for our bondages. I hope we will both be successful, however, in arresting our problems. *That*, we can take steps to do.

I think of an arrested bondage as a sleeping wild animal. Much as we would like to kill the animal, it is possible only to put him to sleep. Asleep, he does not trouble us. We are free from him and can function normally. It only takes one good kick in the ribs of the sleeping animal, however, to quickly arouse all the old ferocity and destructiveness.

Our bondages remain, therefore, howbeit in a dormant state. I think it is a divine arrangement which keeps our bondages with us but in a dormant state. For one thing, it reminds us from whence we have come. We once lay helpless in the gutter of our lives, and but for the grace of God, we would still be there.

What does one do with his bondages? What steps can one take to enter into freedom? Four suggestions:

a. *Claim your bondage(s).* Admit and accept. We have already talked sufficiently about this.

b. *Kiss your chains, and they will become a key.* This idea comes from the life of a very courageous Frenchman Pierre D'Harcourt, who was in the French underground during World War II. Somehow he was betrayed, and after a gun battle in which he was wounded, Pierre was taken captive and thrown into prison. He wrote:

> Before I knew what had happened, they had handcuffed both my hands to the iron frame of the bed.
>
> The hour which followed was one of the blackest of my life. How could I get through the night stretched out in this position? If I had let myself go and struggled, perhaps I would have driven myself mad by the next morning. It was clear that my plot (to escape) had been discovered. And as I realized my chance had gone, despair came over me. For a long time I lay with dry eyes, turning over in my mind every possibility of getting out alive and assessing the chances. Having made every sort of calculation, having peered into all the slightest possibilities, I saw that it was hopeless. At that, something gave way inside me. Left utterly alone with

the wreck of my plans, I did what I should have done before, I turned my face to God and asked for help.

It is difficult to describe exactly what I felt. Beneath everything, beyond everything, I felt myself humiliated and defeated. I had been so confident, and now my pride had been laid low. There was only one way of coming to terms with my fate if I was not to sink into an abyss of defeatism from which I knew I could never rise again. I must make the gesture of complete humility by offering to God all that I suffered. I must not only have the courage to accept the suffering He had sent me; I must also thank Him for it, for the opportunity He gave me to find at last His truth and love. I remember the relief of weeping as I realized that this was my salvation. Then the inspiration came to me to kiss the chains which held me prisoner, and with much difficulty I at last managed to do this. I am not a credulous person, but even allowing for the state of mind I was in that night, there can be no doubt in my mind that some great power from outside momentarily entered into me. Once my lips had touched the steel I was freed from the terror which possessed me. As the handcuffs had brought the terror of death to me, now by kissing my manacles I had turned them from bonds into a key. . . . In the blackness of that night my faith gave me light. Peace returned to me and I slept quietly, accepting death which would bring me life.

c. *Let go of the bondage . . . let God handle it.* By letting go, we mean that we no longer fight it. No longer do we assault the problem and try to overcome it in our own strength; we turn the problem over to God for solution.

Our bondages are more than we can cope with. It is only sensible, therefore, that we should stop the "I-will-power" approach to our problem and call in Someone who is a higher power—God.

To be sure, that creates a crisis in itself: if God is

invited in, He comes in as Number One because that is what He is. This means I must resign as Number One and become a Number Two. This is agony to the egoist. He suffers—yes, must even die. The only immediate compensation we can give him is that the dying unto self is not nearly so painful as the suffering he will endure if he continues as Number One. So we have a choice of sufferings. To remain an egoist and live in bondage is terribly painful. To choose to die to self is also painful, *but not for long,* because God's freedom, peace, and joy will make us "more than conquerors."

Just this morning, I received a letter from a man who was a former mental patient. I came to know him intimately during his illness. He displayed strong psychotic symptoms, was episodically suicidal, withdrawn, and worrisome. Listen to parts of his letter:

> Right now I am so full that I truly *feel* my cup is running over. More and more I am finding it easier to let go. . . . I was saying, "I will to do"—but I realize I should be saying, "I'm willing to let go." . . . I really want to be taught this new way. . . . My entire family is changing. . . . I only hope that more people will find this new way.

The new way is very old. Jesus Christ taught us this new way.

The new way is for *every* human bondage, not just "religious problems."

The new way is for *everyone,* not just a few perceptive people.

d. *Remain under the rule of the Kingdom of God.*

I made the point before that God arrests but does not cure our bondages. That almost sounds as if God does a shoddy job of saving us. Nothing like that was intended. I simply meant that an alcoholic, for example, once God has freed him from the bondage of alcohol-

---

*Pierre D'Harcourt, *The Real Enemy* (New York: Scribners, 1967) pp. 42-43 ism, cannot return to social drinking. The arrested alcoholic cannot so much as take one drink without plunging himself headlong into his old prison of alcohol. Once an alcoholic, always. What is true for alcoholism, holds true for all bondages.

If it is true that bondages are arrested rather than cured, it follows that we will need to stay under a continuous discipline to maintain our freedom. By a "continuous discipline," I mean an authority-structure which can represent God to us, for God Himself is the key to freedom. This is the whole idea behind the Christian church, though it is rare today to see it function as an instrument for inner freedom. But ideally, the church is a loving discipline invited over us by one who affirms Jesus Christ as Lord. Such a church cares for, admonishes, trains, and counsels its membership. Note especially, however, that one never outgrows the need for such a program. No one ever finishes going to church. We note, in passing, that psychotherapy claims to reach a termination point—one based, I feel, on the erroneous assumption that our bondages can be cured.

3. *The Belly of Hell.*
Out of the belly of Sheol (death) I cried. . . . (Jon. 2:2)

Life in the Kingdom of Self adds up to only one thing—suffering.

Eventually, the cup of suffering overflows in the lives of each one of us. We hit bottom.

A new friend of mine has told me how he came to have six livid scars on his left wrist. "I was bursting with anger and despair. This was the end. I grabbed the razor and began slashing myself, but the sight of blood brought me to my senses. I cried out, 'God, you go to hell! Oh, Jesus Christ help me!' Then I slept. When I awoke, the first thought in my mind was to go to a hospital." This is one man's description of being in the belly of death.

Most of us stop short of attempted suicide, but there are few of us who do not at some point in our lives reach the end. Pierre D'Harcourt described his end as "hopeless. At that, something gave way inside me. I was left utterly alone with the wreck of my plans."

A married couple reached out to me for help some time ago. The husband is debonair and exudes self-confidence. He is successful in the business world. I am sure a battery of psychological tests would show this man to be strong, while his wife appears to be weak. She has numerous bondages—countless fears, inability to do her work, hiding from life by staying in bed all day, suspicion, and suicidal tendencies. Add to this, however, one thing: she is at her end. She is sated with suffering.

In the course of our counseling session, the husband complained that his wife no longer cooked his favorite dishes. The wife, in turn, complained that she was no longer taken out to her favorite restaurants. As I heard these complaints, I decided to ask each to "give in" on these small issues.

The wife immediately complied. She was willing to do anything that would help. I turned to her husband and soon learned that all his "strength" was weakness. He saw no reason to take her out to eat, since he felt no love for his wife. Besides, he was not the problem. It was his wife who was breaking down—and he rattled on, ad infinitum. His decision: no eating out. The wife decided to serve him his favorite dishes nonetheless.

This wise woman was in better shape in her brokenness than her husband in all his glorious strength. She is very close to the Kingdom of God, for she has the necessary qualifications of brokenness, poverty, and desperation. This is why the Beatitudes bless those in poverty, persecution, and mourning. They are the only ones who are ready to leave the Kingdom of Self. They are at the end of their ropes. They have spent their last buck and shot their last bullet. To all such people, our Lord says, "Congratulations! Because you have lost everything and are so wretchedly poor, you are now in position to leave the Kingdom of Self and enter the Kingdom of God" (cf. Matt. 5:3).

Sometimes I think my mental-patient parishioners have a great advantage over us so-called mentally healthy people. At least many of my patients know they have problems. Moreover, they are oftentimes ready to do anything to find a solution. They will even go to the extent of accepting God into their lives! It is suffering people who come to God. They come, not because it is a nice idea or because they feel like it, but because their suffering is so intense they will be killed by their pain if they do not come. So thank God for pain and suffering, else few of us would find Him.

When does one reach a bottom? Where is that point at which the cup of suffering overflows? That point is reached when one *says* he has reached it. The point of surrender is different for each person. One is well-advised, however, to say, "I have *had* it," as quickly as possible.

> Why will you die, O house of Israel? For I have no pleasure in the death of any one, says the Lord God; so turn, and live. (Ezek. 18:31-32)

As freely as one is able to declare his contentment with whatever the degree of his blessings, so we are free to declare our readiness for God at whatever point of suffering we find ourselves.

This strange paradox—that only the End brings the Beginning, that suffering must precede our joy, that we must die before we live—is nowhere better illustrated than with God. God, in a certain sense, knows the taste of failure. His "failure" with the Jews is recorded in detail in the Old Testament. He "failed" in the eyes of the world as He hung on the cross.

God's "failures" are apparently shown for no other reason than to welcome us "failures" into His fellowship of suffering, so that we may share the delight of His eternal victory and success.

I doubt very much whether this book will mean very much to people who have not done their share of suffering. The positions taken in this book are all formed in the crucible of my own suffering. My prayer is that my suffering will connect with yours and that together we may rejoice in the fantastic way in which God has turned our sorrow into joy and our weeping into shouts of laughter.

Let us now turn to some unbelievably good news. The good news of the Kingdom of God is too good to believe. If it were not so good as it is, more people would believe it and buy it. Those who reject the Kingdom of God can do so only on the grounds that it offers too much rather than too little. So let us look at what our Lord taught concerning the Kingdom of God.

5

The Kingdom of God—A Summary of Christ's Teachings

The kingdom of heaven is at hand. (Matt. 10:7)

The Kingdom of Heaven, the Kingdom of Christ, the Kingdom of God—these are all the same Kingdom. It was called the Kingdom of Heaven in deference to many Jews who were averse to speaking the divine name, lest His holy name be made common or possibly be profaned. The Kingdom is Christ's because Christ is God's Son, and, therefore, He is heir to the Kingdom. This Kingdom is God's, and He is the rightful King not only because He alone is divine, but because His subjects have freely invited Him to rule over them.

I hasten to add, however, that He chose us as His subjects long before we chose Him as our king. He led us to Himself with an utterly uncoerced coercion. God did this and is doing it today through the cross—His and ours. The demonstrated love of Christ dying as an atonement for our sins evokes our love. But God is also drawing us to Him through the suffering of our personal crosses. When the deadly cup of suffering finally kills off all intention of self-rule, we are made ready for the rule of God.

The twelve disciples, and later a group of seventy followers, were sent out to proclaim the reign of this Sovereign. Christ sent them to the lost sheep of the house of Israel (Matt. 10:6). Why them? They understood. They were ready right now. Christ's message to them was this: "My Kingdom is also right now. It's here."

For us today, the Kingdom of God is also at hand. I understand this to mean that we should not think of the Kingdom of God as some past or future event. Nor should we think of it as something which we must bring into our lives by hard work. Everything has been done. The Kingdom of God is now, at the very moment you are reading these words.

I had a dream which made all this clear to me.

In my dream, I had been invited to speak at a weekend retreat, and I chose to speak on the Kingdom of God. At the close of the conference, we had a banquet. The chairman spoke with appreciation and enthusiasm about my earlier presentation. This surprised me because, frankly, it was not that good. What surprised me even more in this dream was when the chairman asked me to rise and say a few more words about the Kingdom.

As I got to my feet, the strangest thing happened. I saw a vision in my dream. The heavens rolled back like a curtain, and what I saw revealed will never be forgotten. A trumpet blew and a voice announced, "In My Father's house are many mansions!" I then saw a city—a very clean city. It was indescribably beautiful. The mansions were made of brick with lovely red tile roofs. It was a city set on sloping hills, and again I noticed how clean it all was.

I could not contain my excitement and so, turning to my audience, I cried, "Do you see it? This is the Kingdom of God! It's here—right now! Don't you see it?"

They did not. They were laughing at me as they walked out of the banquet hall. As the retreatants left, I overheard one say to his friend, "The man is crazy! It's a good thing he works in a mental hospital. He needs help."

And then I awoke—agreeing with them, and also laughing with them. Because I know very well how crazy it is to speak of the Kingdom of God as being here, right now.

The Kingdom of God is within you. (Luke 17:21 KJV)

When a person in his heart says "Lord" to Jesus Christ, the Kingdom of God exists. To say that, however, presupposes that one no longer says "Lord" to oneself in the Kingdom of Self. This is all an internal arrangement. The kingdoms both of God and man are within man.

There is a God-created throne in the heart of every man. That throne is intended for God alone, and yet without exception, every man enthrones himself, and then, as a penalty for insurrection against the Almighty, earns death. "The wages of sin is death" (Rom. 6:23). Sin is self-enthronement in one's heart long before it is externalized in specific unlawful acts. "For out of the heart proceed evil thoughts, murders, adulteries, fornications, thefts, false witness, blasphemies" (Matt. 15:19 KJV). Now if the wages of sin is death, then the wages of Christ as King of one's heart is life. These kingdoms are within us.

We can, on this basis, account for the natural antagonism which we, in our egocentric state, feel toward God. The reason so many fear God in childhood and hate Him in adulthood, is because He is seen as a pretender to the throne on which self rules. God is the Enemy. It does no good to tell the person who holds this conviction that God loves Him. No! He feels God hates him, and he hates God. What may help such a person, however, is to explain that in the scheme of his own thinking, in the system of values he holds, there is no place for God because the person himself insists on playing god. This god-playing takes place in his heart. The contest between the kings takes place within us—because that is where the kingdoms are located.

The kingdom of heaven is like a grain of mustard seed. (Matt. 13:31)

The beginning of the reign of God in a human heart is so inauspicious, so paltry and small, that it is frequently unnoticeable. Even when it is observed, it is difficult to believe that from this tiny seed of faith, a great tree of life will develop. I know from my work as a chaplain that many of my parishioners have entered into the Kingdom of God in a very simple manner. For many of these people, the journey to the Kingdom of God was begun with the simple step of asking for an appointment. I recall a man who casually remarked, "Sometime I'd like to sit down with you and talk a little." Since it could hardly be said that he was storming the gates of God's Kingdom, I decided to test his intentions. I simply took out my datebook and asked, "Shall we set a time?" My friend, somewhat compliantly, set a time.

Who would ever expect that anything worthwhile would ever come from such a poor beginning? I was even more doubtful after our first hour together, because all he wanted to tell me was that his wife was a first-class witch. Toward the end of that hour, however, I was able to share one or two impressions with him: I noted his strong tendencies to both judge and then execute his wife, explaining that this violent and fruitless way of relating to his wife was a piece of his long-used egocentric pattern of life. He understood. He also understood when I explained a new option to him: theocentric life in the Kingdom of God.

"I have a suggestion," I continued. "Take a walk. Think it over. If you want to continue on your present basis, I'll accept that. If you are ready for life in the Kingdom of God, come back and tell me. Either way, we will always be fast friends."

My friend left. I prayed. Less than an hour later, he returned to say simply and softly, "I'm ready."

I know that with those two words he had crossed the threshold into the Kingdom of God, and yet, it was such a small beginning. There remained acre upon acre of unsurrendered territory in his life. All we presently had were words—only two at that—and no deeds. But that is the way the Kingdom of God, it seems, always begins. Like a tiny mustard seed.

The kingdom of heaven is like unto treasure hid in a field. (Matt. 13:44 KJV)

Jesus told a story about a man who was walking across a field when suddenly he stopped dead in his tracks. There, through a crack in the ground, he could see a treasure chest. It took only a little digging to uncover it. He hoisted the chest out of the hole, opened its lid and—to his utter amazement—beheld ancient treasures of gold, silver, and jewelry in such abundance that no estimate could be placed on the cache!

The excited man quickly looked around to see if anyone might have observed this discovery. No one had. He immediately buried the treasure once again and literally ran to a local real estate office. The price on that particular parcel of land was very high. It would require selling his home and business, as well as borrowing a considerable sum. I suspect that the realtor was surprised over the readiness with which his client agreed to the price. Neither did he seem the least depressed over selling his home and business. Strange.

But not strange to our new millionaire. No sooner was the deal completed than he was back in the field, digging, with a big smile on his face. And there it was! —the treasure was right where he had left it. Now it was his!

The search for riches was finished. He had them in hand. His heart was filled with joy.

This is a parable—slightly embellished—of the King-dom of God.

Our treasure is a Person—God. This treasure is not an idea, an explanation, nor an analysis. The answers to life's problems are not in theology, nor in philosophy, nor in the sciences. The best these can do is present us with words and ideas. Only a Person—one whom we call God—can satisfy our needs, answer our problems, and end our search. *He* is the Answer. The "it" answers are no answers.

This Answer brings joy. Leon Bloy has said, "The most infallible proof of the presence of God in a person is joy." Someone else has said, "Joy is the flag we fly from the castle-towers of our hearts when the Lord-King is in residence."

Once we realize that the treasured Person has been found, it begins to register with us that our long search for something lost, something missing, is finished. St. Augustine said it long ago: "Our hearts cannot repose, O Lord, until they rest in Thee."

Unless you turn and become like children, you will never enter the kingdom of heaven. (Matt. 18:3)

"Whoever humbles himself like this child, he is the greatest in the kingdom of heaven" (Matt. 18:4). Little children are humble-minded (occasionally, when their egoism permits) because their store of knowledge is so scanty. This makes them open—open to mystery, paradox; indeed, to whatever is taught them. Adults, who have spent years laboriously building a system of knowledge which they have labeled "truth," are open only to ideas which coincide with and enhance their present stockpile of learning. After years of building this monument to ourselves, some of us found that the whole effort was a waste of time. We were humbled by the results of our own folly—and finally, ready for the Source of Truth, God.

Leo Tolstoy, at the age of fifty, found that he had to become a child willing to be taught by some very humble teachers. Of him, Ernest J. Simmons writes:

Since the faith of worldly theologians and of the people of his own class repelled him, Tolstoy turned to believers among the poor, simple, unlettered folk: pilgrims, monks, sectarians and peasants. . . . The life of his own spoiled and rich circle had lost all meaning for him, but the life of the laboring people, of the great masses of mankind that produce life, now appeared to him in its true light. . . . The humble people of Russia had led Tolstoy to an understanding of the meaning of life and to a belief in God.*

When I entered the mental hospital chaplaincy, I was told that I was well-trained for my work. I, too, believed this. I had taken the right courses, gotten the best training, received the proper accreditation. I set to work with vigor. The results were disastrous. What had been taught me was not really helping people, and in some cases, it was adding to their problems. I was in a state of despair, ready to quit both the hospital and the ministry.

It was at that point that God turned me to some recovered alcoholic patients. These men had no degrees, no training in counseling—all they had was sobriety. I was struck also by the fact that they were quiet inside. I was not. It was at the feet of these broken people that I first began to learn. They taught me at the age of thirty-eight my first lessons about a living God—after I had been in the ministry nine years.

Leave the dead to bury their own dead; but as for you, go and proclaim the kingdom of God. (Luke 9:60)

That means obedience. Obedience, that is, to terms other than our own. The obedience is to the King. This terminates the rule of Self.

Note that this obedience is not a feeling of agreement but rather an act of submission to the King, often in spite of one's disagreement. In the above passage of

*Ernest J. Simmons, *Leo Tolstoy* (New York: Vintage Books, 1960), Vol. 1, pp. 360,370.

Scripture, our Lord faced a man who wished to follow Him. Christ wanted the man's services immediately. The man, however, wished to return home to bury his father. The would-be follower would not defer to Christ. His obedience was only a nice idea. When it came to action (which is what really counts in obedience), he held back. The only kind of obedience the King accepts, however, is the kind which goes into action.

But surely not just any kind of action we might choose. There are multitudes of religious people in the world who right this moment are knocking themselves out with their good deeds, their philanthropies, and their religious rituals. Good as these self-chosen acts are, if they are not preceded by the act of surrender of the will to God's rule, the doer is working himself into a terrible delusion. God does not want our service. He wants our obedience. That means the unconditional surrender of ourselves on God's terms, not ours.

The need for surrender first and service second is clearly taught in Jesus' encounter with the rich young ruler. This man kept the commandments perfectly, but when our Lord suggested new terms, namely, that he sell all his possessions and follow Christ, the young man turned away in sorrow. He was prepared only to work hard for God, not to surrender and become obedient, for that would mean an end to living on his own terms.

The decision to act out our obedience to Christ does not require that our feelings be in full support of the act. Indeed, if we wait for our fickle feelings to endorse the commands of Christ, He will never become our Leader. Even the initial act of surrender to Christ need not be sponsored by feelings of glad willingness. The only thing necessary is that we capitulate, regardless of how we feel about it. God only wants our weapons on the table. He does not care how we feel about surrendering them. The rich young ruler was only asked to surrender. He was not asked to like it.

So this is the order—an act of obedience first, and then the feelings will eventually follow. The whole world wants that order reversed. People want to feel like doing something before they act. Christ rejects this nugget of human wisdom.

How can we go into action in obeying God?

A large part of our obedience to God is actualized through the instruments of human authority—such as laws, institutions, and role people. Paul tells us, "Let every person be subject to the governing authorities" (Rom. 13:1). Peter adds, "Be subject for the Lord's sake to every human institution" (I Pet. 2:13). We are counseled to obey God through surrogate authority except when such authority conflicts with our obedience to God. At such time, we are to obey God rather than man.

Normally, we think of human authority as being vested in law and government, but I think of it here in a much wider sense. Obedience is also expressed through "role people," such as pastors, medical doctors, foremen, AA sponsors, etc. Indeed, a person can authorize *anyone* to function as a representative of God to him.

If you and I were together, and I was burdened with a sense of guilt, would you not hear my confession in confidence if I asked this of you? And would you not assure me, as God's spokesman, that I am pardoned? If my guilt was the result of stealing something from a store, would you not also suggest that I return the stolen article? Now that suggestion means new terms. My terms are to keep the goods. You bring new terms, God's terms. If I accept those terms, I become obedient. You, then, are an agent of God to me.

An older friend of mine has a real hang-up with watching sports on TV. He is drawn like a magnet, especially to the body-contact sports—boxing, football, and hockey. This fellow got so emotionally involved in these programs that his fists, shoulders, and entire body were all in movement as he watched the programs. His family laughed at him and treated the matter lightly.

My friend, however, did not laugh, nor did he feel at all complacent about his sports craze. He knew he was addicted to violence, that he experienced strong feelings of guilt after these programs, that he was wasting his time, that he could not break free from his compulsive TV-watching, and that God wanted very much for him to be free from this bondage. It was a serious problem with him, and he knew it.

One day—when he finally had reached THE END, he said to his wife, "Honey, I've *had* it with these programs. Could you and I sit down once a week to decide which programs to avoid and which to see? And then, would you hold me to it?" His wife agreed.

Their agreement worked—immediately! A fundamental spiritual law in the Kingdom of God had been set in operation—namely, that the obedient person becomes the free person.

Obedience to God through people is also expressed in a Christian's compassion for broken people. If our help to suffering people is based on humanistic ideals or the lovableness of those who suffer, we will soon turn away, because the helpers are all too ego-involved, and the helped are often very unlovable. There needs to be a better reason for helping people than people. Compassion based on obedience to God is the only way our actions can have real meaning.

Repent ye: for the kingdom of heaven is at hand.
(Matt. 3:2 KJV)

Before one can be born anew into the Kingdom, one must first repent. Repentance means that one has a change of heart. Phillips translates this passage, "You must change your hearts—for the kingdom of Heaven has arrived!"

Repentance, therefore, goes far beyond sorrow over sins we have committed. When John the Baptist spoke these words, he had in mind the deepest possible change in a person—the change resulting from an invitation to God to take up residence in the human heart.

That change is so drastic in the human heart that at first it registers as one's death sentence. I suppose that is why the Bible speaks of "dying to self." The self, however, does not really die. The self "dies" only as to his egocentric position in the world. We were positioned squarely in the center of our world, and of course, that meant that God (as Jesus Christ, the Son of God) had to die—which He did in actual fact as a means of confirming what every man does to the divine Christ. In a real sense, we all killed Christ, because whenever we live the egocentric life, Christ is dead to us. But when Christ lives in us, then the self takes its rightful subordinate position.

Love one another. (John 15:17)

Judge not. (Matt. 7:1)

Do not resist one who is evil. If anyone strikes you on the right cheek, turn to him the other also. (Matt. 5:39)

Love your enemies. (Matt. 5:44)

Christ gave us only one commandment to follow. He did not command us to be good, right, knowledgeable, nor did He command us to be custodians of ultimate truth and manifestations of religious piety. He commands us only to love.

It is always difficult to put into words what our Lord meant by love, but for our purposes, it is sufficient to think of love as a combination of acceptance, caring for another, and the willingness to sacrifice oneself for the sake of the beloved.

We have little trouble with such attitudes as long as the person with whom we are dealing is attractive, responsive, and lovable.

A more difficult test of our acceptance-caring-sacrifice arises when it must practiced as an act of will, simply because the love object is so unattractive and even, at times, repulsive.

The ultimate test of our love, however, is when that unlovable person attacks us. Christ addressed Himself to this problem. He is very clear that we are not to judge our tormentor. We are not to resist one who is evil. And, more positively, we are to love our enemy so that he feels the full force of our acceptance-caring-sacrifice with neither abatement nor termination.

All this brings gloom to the heart of any egoist. He has trained himself from the beginning to retaliate, to trade hate for hate and to escalate the violence. Christ's teaching about non-judgment, non-resistance to evil, and loving the enemy strikes at the very center of our egocentric philosophy of life. Nowhere is our self-life contradicted as flatly and sharply as in these doctrines of Christ. It is important, therefore, that we linger on our Lord's teaching of non-violence for a few moments.

How is a citizen of the Kingdom of God to respond to the attacks, the violence, and the hatred which the enemies of the Kingdom aim at him?

The person under God is to leave all judgment of his enemy to God. The enemy may be dead wrong. Yet God must punish sin. Punishment is not a function of man. "Vengeance is mine, I will repay, says the Lord" (Rom. 12:19). Nor can the enemy's errors be used to sanction anger and justify retaliation. The man of God realizes that "justifiable resentment" and "righteous indignation" are the worst and most hypocritical forms of anger.

Non-violence toward an enemy, therefore, means much more than refraining from shooting him. It means more, also, than refusing to hate the doer of evil. Ultimately, non-violent love means doing the enemy *good*. Attack him with kindness. "If your enemy is hungry, feed him; if he is thirsty, give him drink" (Rom. 12:20). Difficult as it is, the citizen of the

Kingdom of God seeks positive ways to express acceptance-caring-sacrifice.

The strategy of non-violent love is basically beneficial in at least two ways: (1) It heaps "burning coals" (Rom. 12:20) upon the head of the enemy. That is, the approach educates rather than humiliates. This method holds some hope of enlightening and reforming one's opponent. The way may thus be open for a reconciliation of the parties involved; (2) Non-violence benefits the person who practices it. This simple strategy frees one from resentment. To be free of resentment is to be free of our most damaging emotion. If resentment is allowed to remain in our hearts, it will surely burn a hole in us. What we should do, therefore, is refer our judgment and resentment into the hands of the Judge of all the earth. No one benefits more from this than the non-violent person himself.

In this simple way, a great moral victory is assured us. We do not need, nor do we want that false and foolish "victory" which violence brings. Everyone loses in such a struggle. No one ever wins any kind of a war. Both parties always end in fatigue, the winner being the one who delivers a weak final blow to which his weakened opponent is unable to respond. Any victory by physical or verbal force is no victory. A moral victory is assured the person who practices non-violence. If his "opponent" is humbled in the face of this moral force, he is then invited to share in this victory. Behold—*two* winners.

I think I speak the mind of the King in suggesting the following steps in the non-violent approach to human problems:

a. Take your stand, not because you are always right, but because you humbly wish to place yourself on the side of God's truth, law, and love.

b. Explain your position to your "opponent." Never mind knocking his position. He has a perfect right to his opinion. So do you. Explain it to him.

c. Give up your "opponent" to God. Let go . . . let

God. Let God judge and change the other person. When we grab these functions, we leave no room for God. Our Lord told us what to do with our enemies. We are to pray for them, that their hearts and lives may be changed.

d. *If attacked, love your enemy.* This sounds like a paradox but it works. You are not up against a deep-eyed villain but only a man who has done wrong. Even though you are striving to undo the wrong, show good will to him no matter what he does. Do not vilify, ridicule or humiliate him at any time, in any way. Let him know at all times that you are out to establish justice, not to defeat him.*

e. *Keep working on your own problems.* We have plenty to do improving ourselves. He who forgets this soon becomes a messianic egoist who spends all his energy leading lost souls into a promised land about which he himself knows nothing.

We should be aware that the principle of non-violence can be misused and twisted like anything else God has given us. Non-violence can feed the martyr complex in a dependent, passive personality. Martyrism is obviously an ego-trip in which a person uses suffering to gain glory. The correction needed by such a person, however, is *not* to stand up and slug it out. Characteristically, egocentrics either fight or run— which is precisely what the belligerent attacker wants. What *is* needed is for the egoistic martyr to take his stand and then return good for evil.

The way of non-violence, though it will certainly save our souls from hatred, never guarantees us that we will be free from physical harm. Jesus Christ died on a cross. You and I may be asked to make a similar sacrifice if we follow in His footsteps.

How to Practice Non-Violence, published by the Fellowship of Reconciliation, Box 271, Nyack, N. Y. These five suggestions borrow heavily from this brochure.

On second thought, however, holding to non-violence to the end is not at all a bad way to end our days, if God so wills. What better way to die than faithful to God's eternal cause? Dying for that cause certainly beats dying in a hospital bed with all those medical technicians frantically trying to get a little more mileage out of us. May the Lord spare us from such an unhappy ending! Dying for the cause of Christ far surpasses meeting my Maker on a battlefield, engaged in a foolish war which should never have been started in the first place. And if I have a choice between suffering physical harm as a result of practicing non-violence or suffering physical harm as a result of colliding with a drunken driver on a highway, I know which I would choose. Or, again, what comparison is there between suffering from heart disease and suffering for the cause of righteousness and truth? God may ask us to do both, but still, nothing else can give our lives real meaning as much as obeying Christ. If such obedience means death, it will be a death which will crown our lives with meaning and purpose.

In summary, there are two kingdoms: the Kingdom of Self and the Kingdom of God. If God's kingdom becomes established in the human heart, it is hardly noticed at first, because we allow God only the smallest control over our wills. King Self surrenders by degrees. Ego-slaying and obedience are terribly painful, and yet afterward there is a quality of inexpressible joy which the presence of God generates in us. It is a law of the Kingdom of God that we must lose all to find Him. We must die to our egocentrism to be born anew into the eternal Kingdom. Finally, to live under the King who is God, means to live *with* other persons in a loving, non-violent style of life.

"If I receive God into my life," a man once asked me, "will He overwhelm me? Will He take more than I am willing to give?"

I assured my worried friend that God, on entering our hearts, does not crush our wills. We retain the

6

The Kingdom of God Is the Kingdom
of Right Relationships

1. The Individual in Relation to Himself.

Once the Rule of God is established in the human heart, that person becomes free from the tyranny of himself. I know that such a statement may sound like a cliché and an over-simplification of human problems, but thousands of freed people are today rejoicing in the reality and victory of this *simple* understanding of life. Anyone, you well know, can make things complex. The whole world applauds complex solutions. We should be finished with complex solutions, not because they do not entertain our minds, but because they do not work. We should work hard to make things more simple. It is not easy, but we can be cheered by the advice of those who encourage us to KISS—meaning: "Keep it simple, Stupid!"

The simple truth is that the self positioned as god is the basic cause of the entire gamut of emotional problems in people. What we commonly call neuroses, psychoses, addiction problems, and behavior problems are the results of a life wrongly set up. It is time to abandon the complex explanations which the professional experts in our culture hand us. Emotional problems are not caused first of all by traumatic events in childhood, nor by a faulty environment, nor heredity, nor by the defects of our parents' training. What seems much closer to the truth is that we quickly used these events in our past to further establish our egoistic way of life. We used whatever happened to us to further get our way.

Not only do we "use" our histories and environments as "reasons" for our present behavior, but we also use whatever emotional bondage has accrued to further our egoistic way of life. To illustrate: Here is a middle-aged woman who is chronically ill. Her problems range from migraine headaches to upset stomach, from palpitation of the heart to skin rashes. She told me she was aware of what caused all this. It was her unhappy marriage. She had married the wrong man, and for twenty years her life had been hell. There was no doubt in her mind about the cause of her problem. It was sitting at home right now looking at TV—another thing she could not stand.

As the woman went on with her story, she revealed that she had used this husband as the excuse for building and unloading tons of resentment which, I gently pointed out, was nothing but a monument to her own egoism. The cause of her egoism was further supported by her near-total absorption in herself. She spent most of her waking hours nursing herself back to health, spending money on herself at the doctor, and if there was any time remaining, she would worry about what her next illness might be. This is the hallmark of an egoist—a nearly total self-absorption, based solely on one's pathetic emotional bondage.

The reason for this self-absorption is well-founded: It is a massive effort to fight off death. Death is at work in the hypochondriac—just as death is at work in an alcoholic, a suicidal person, a work-maniac who earns a heart attack, a law-breaker who goes to prison, or a drug addict. In all these problems, there is a frantic intent to shed the body, to get rid of it, to die. All bondage impells us in the direction of death. The self in control of the self seeks to kill himself. The wages of god-playing is eventually the destruction of the self, which is what I think Paul had in mind when he said, "The wages of sin is death" (Rom. 6:23).

Why should god-playing end in death?

Is it not because god-playing is so unnatural to man? Being ultimate goes so contrary to man's *intended* nature, that every fiber of his being rises up in massive protest. Playing god is as unnatural to man as trying to fly like a bird simply because a person knows how to swing his arms. That man will die who jumps off a cliff pretending to be a bird. The price of such a fantasy is death. So with the self who knows no authority over himself except himself.

If our understanding is correct, then we would expect to see in the lives of people-made-Number-Two-by-virtue-of-God-being-their-Number-One, a freedom from the tyranny of the self, various crippling emotional bondages, and the death process working in them.

Miracle of miracles! This is exactly what happens when the surrendered self enters the Kingdom of God. I *know* it is too much to believe. Only fools do. But the lives of many people who have come into this freedom testify to us that our understanding is correct. I say, their *lives* testify to this. We are not interested in clever hypotheses or neat explanations. Shattered people have suffered sufficiently from the glib talkers and that multitude of "healers" who know all the answers but never set us on a course of healing, much less find healing for themselves. When we turn, therefore, to the lives of people who have entered the Kingdom of God, we find that they are a new breed of inwardly free people.

Gert Behanna, among many thousands of case histories, will serve as a clear example. The only child of a Scotch immigrant who became a millionaire, she lived life to the hilt. The price tag on her self-centered, profligate life was staggering: alcoholism, drug addiction, three broken marriages, and attempted suicide. Sunk to the depths of moral and physical misery, her body wracked by psychosomatic illnesses, Gert Behanna had reached the bottom. "I wanted extinction because I was without hope."

A physician advised psychiatry, but strangely, Gert knew what she needed. "I don't need a psychiatrist. What I need is God." To which the doctor replied, "Well, God wouldn't hurt a bit."

A bit later, she read an article by Sam Shoemaker entitled, "It Is Never Too Late to Start Over." Gert went over to her bed and got on her knees.

"God, if you are anywhere around, I wish you would please help me because I sure need it."

In twenty minutes it was all over. It was a spiritual showerbath. I felt cleansed. I felt welcomed. I'd never had a home, and I never made one, but I felt welcomed. I also felt forgiven. I knew exactly who this was—God.

I said, "Thank you very much, Sir. I'll have to start from scratch but I'll tell you one thing: I'll never take another drop of liquor in my life." And I have not.

I started from scratch. I prayed, "Our Father who art—" Then I stopped. Our Father—not theirs—ours. Suddenly I was a sister to everybody. Suddenly I thought about my own sex. With the thought of women, I thought about cooking, which I knew nothing about. Calling my book dealer in Chicago, I said, "Mr. Chandler, I want a Bible and a copy of *The Joy of Cooking*."

"My God, what's happened to you?" asked Mr. Chandler.

"My God has happened to me," I said, and He had.*

In Gert Behanna's fifty-third year, she discovered that God was not dead, and that through the miracle of Christ's love and power, drugs, liquor, and despair itself could be conquered. In her book, *The Late Liz*, Gert says, "In standing aside and looking back at this woman I used to be, it is more and more possible to detach myself, to view her in third person. She was she, and I am I; Siamese twins perhaps, one of whom must die that the other may live."

A person comes into relationship with himself by coming into a relationship with God. By making God the ultimate authority and power in one's life, the self discovers who he is. The answer to the lifelong question, "Who am I?" is finally answered. I am a human being, created by God—that is who I am. The search for my identity is ended. No longer am I tyrannized and terrorized by myself. Now I live under the love of God in the Kingdom of God. The discovery of God as King invariably brings about a simultaneous discovery of oneself. Formerly, we knew ourselves as a goddish being and hated ourselves for it. Now we know ourselves as human beings.

2. *The Individual in Relation to His Spouse.*

Let us talk for a moment about the idea of marriage. The divine intention is that husband and wife are basically equal as persons, for how else can they be united in one flesh? These persons of equal worth are meant to complement each other in a relationship in which they are to "be subject to one another out of reverence for Christ" (Eph. 5:21). Ideally, each spouse would then care as much for the needs of the other as for his own desires.

That such a marriage is a rarity, none will deny. There is a simple and accurate explanation for this:

*"God Isn't Dead!" by Gert Behanna (Waco, Texas: Word Records Incorporated).

85

each party in marriage tends toward self-centeredness. Egocentrism destroys marriage. Husbands and wives who play god on each other can hardly avoid a tiring, fruitless, marital war.

Since it is difficult for the husband and wife to equally play god on each other at the same time, what usually happens is that first one will play god and then the other.

I know of a man who, soon after marriage, sent his wife out of the kitchen because he knew more than she about cooking. He was not satisfied with the way she was doing it, so he took over. In addition, this fellow would never allow his wife or children to buy clothes unless he was in the store to approve their purchases. Even worse, he actually selected the clothes he wished his wife to wear. We can understand the complaint of his wife when she shouted, "You are nothing but a dictator! You and Hitler belong together!"

After about five years of marriage, they both became so sick of it that one day the husband announced, "I've had it! From now on, you can have charge of the whole family. You worry about us from now on."

And would you believe it? From that day, the wife wore the pants. When finally the husband arrived at my study, he was complaining that he felt like "the fifth and last child in the family."

From this example, we can learn that the relationship of egoists in marriage can and does change. In this particular marriage, the husband became a Christian, whereupon his egocentric wife left him and eventually ended the marriage. Had the husband remained egocentric, I expect there would have been an accommodation, and some kind of a marriage would have continued. What we pray for, of course, is that both parties will come under the rule of Christ and then enter Christian marriage—which is the only kind that really works.

The real unity in a marriage must come on the spiritual level if it is to be a true marriage. Until the husband and wife meet under God, they will relate only on the level of self-interest, competition, and eventual estrangement, though not necessarily separation or divorce.

Though the husband and wife are equal, we must also recognize, however, a difference of function in the marriage. Because a husband is given the function of leadership and ultimate responsibility, Paul enjoins wives to be subject to their husbands as to the Lord (Eph. 5:22). All Paul is saying here is that you cannot have four hands on the steering wheel of the family car. It is best if the husband steers and the wife assists him with the no less important functions of map-reading and controlling the children. It is true, the husband may ask his wife to drive the car for a time, in which case the wife has control of the car, but even then, she should not be given the power to make final decisions. This power must remain with one person—the husband —because if it is passed back and forth, no one knows what his role is in the dangerous crises of life.

In Christian marriage, a wife does not hesitate to be subject to her husband, because she realizes that he, as well as she, is under the authority of Christ. Were the husband to revert back to an egocentric life-style, the wife would be understandably concerned about a dictatorial use of power upon her, but this should not deter her from playing her God-given role as a wife.

The proof of the husband's submission to Christ can be seen in the desire to love his wife. Surely this means he would be sensitive to her needs. It also means that the husband would invite and give full weight to the wife's feelings and opinions in all decision-making. But loving a wife means more. When Paul urged husbands to "love your wives" (Eph. 5:25), he also intended that a husband should never enforce or coerce his decisions upon his wife. A husband is given authority to lead, but no authority to force his wife to follow. In this, a husband follows the example of his Lord who, though He gave us the Ten Commandments, never forces us to obey them. On the wife's part, when she freely chooses to be subject to her husband, she does it as an act of obedience to Christ rather than to her husband.

It hardly needs to be added that Christian marriage is a solemn, permanent covenant. Whoever breaks that covenant by adultery or desertion is in conflict with God. That places many people in conflict with God today, because the institution of marriage is in terrible distress, due largely to the accelerating egocentrism flourishing in our culture. And still, I have never seen a troubled marital relationship which could not have been healed by the simple grace of forgiveness. But forgiveness is abhorrent to one who is playing the judge.

Here again, the only solution is God, because He alone is the Judge. His judgment is far more merciful than that of the warring partners in marriage. A healthy marital relationship will not become sick, nor will a marriage covenant be broken, as long as a central place is given God in the marriage.

In summary, when God is invited into a marriage, and the Rule of God takes root, that marriage will grow and become a joy beyond description. Without God, marriage degenerates, because egoists are always antagonists. It's that simple. Let us now look at the two offspring we always see in a marriage of egoists: violence and deprivation.

Violence

Let us think of the most common kinds of violence—physical violence and something that hurts even worse, verbal violence. People who have suffered both kinds have told me that getting hit in the mouth hurts, but nothing can compare to words which are used as knives. Whoever resorts to violence in the marriage relationship is really assaulting God, for to attempt the destruction of another means that we are over another —which only God should be. Indeed, violence presupposes a condemning judgment, as we pointed out previously, which leaves no place for the judgment of God.

The only workable way to overcome the problem of violence in marriage is to openly resign as a god-player. If one of my parishioners tells me he hit his wife in the mouth, knocking her dentures across the room, I suggest: (1) that at a time of his choosing, we get on our knees and he ask God's forgiveness; (2) that he write or speak an apology to his wife with a request for pardon; and (3) if he really means business with his problem of violence, that he tell me when he is prepared to hand over his life to God and avoid a repeat performance of this kind of conduct.

I have observed many times that violence toward others begins when we tire of working on our own problems and begin taking a moral inventory of other people. This is something which only they and God have a right to do. When one person appoints himself to the task of taking another's personal inventory, the self-righteous judge invariably adds punishment to his verdict of guilty.

So much for our problem of inflicting violence on a marriage partner. Where there is a donor, however, there is also a receiver. How does one cope with a violent spouse? We know that in the Kingdom of Self, one deals with violence by returning it in greater measure—the law of the jungle, an eye for an eye, the survival of the fittest, and all that. But how, in the Kingdom of God, do we respond to the violence our marriage partner inflicts on us?

I previously attempted to concretely spell out what it means to live under an ethic of love (see pp. 74-79). In summary, a non-violent citizen of the Kingdom of God attempts to:
a. Take his stand.
b. Explain his position to his "opponent."
c. Give up his "opponent" to God.
d. If attacked, he is prepared to love his "enemy" by
   (1) Not resisting evil, turning the other cheek.

89

(2) Moving in close to his "enemy."

(3) Doing him positive good.

(4) Praying for him.

    e. Keep working on his own problems.

These principles are precisely what we need to govern our response to the violence of a spouse. Let us, therefore, cast out that diabolical nonsense which counsels us to learn how to fight fairly in marriage. Fighters—both fair and unfair—lose. But those who lose to God, win. If we choose the path of non-violence in marriage, we are at least guaranteed that we will have one real winner, and possibly two.

The real winner is that person under God who has followed the counsel of Booker T. Washington: "Let no man pull you so low as to make you hate him." The "enemy" in any marriage loves to provoke the other to anger and hate. Indeed, the "enemy" is boiling with new anger because he has lost his power to make his spouse angry. The non-violent spouse is then accused of refusing to get involved, of weakness, of being sick.

Let it be.

Hold on to God. You will survive as a stronger person if you follow His example of loving the unlovable.

There is hope, too, that your example will serve as a guiding light to a spouse who is stumbling in the darkness of anger and violence.

Deprivation

In addition to the problem of violence, there is also the problem of deprivation in marriage. Again, the parties in marriage both deprive and are deprived.

A working wife may deprive her husband of a good home. There is a kind of woman who feels good only when she is at work. When she returns home to a husband who wants involvement with her, she is either too tired or uninterested. The husband, on the other hand, may deprive a wife of sexual intercourse. I know of a husband whose sexual interests are so tied up with pornography and masturbation that he has come to look upon his wife as a sister.

If one is honest enough to admit that he is a depriving spouse, the only hope is to confess it to God and his marriage partner. Then, come into the Kingdom of God. There is freedom from any problem if one comes under His Rule.

As to being deprived, again, the answer is God. Being deprived provokes our egoism. One woman complained to me that she was deprived of a man in her marriage. Her husband was still a little boy, she complained, who picks his nose in public, calls her "mother," and will not go to sleep without a light on in the bedroom. His behavior infuriates his wife. What is the solution to this problem?

She has yelled and screamed at him. We know, therefore, that he is aware of what he is doing. He has a good memory, so there is no need to remind him again. The infantile behavior, however, persists.

What can be done?

Nothing, humanly.

Power was never given us to change another human being. This wife is trying to do the impossible as she vainly attempts to get her husband to grow a few inches taller. Jesus asks us, "And which of you by being anxious can add one cubit to his stature?" (Matt. 6:27). This heroic woman answers, "I can! I can make this immature husband grow up."

But she cannot.

The most helpful thing she can do for her husband is to pray for him. God will have to change him. She cannot.

The wife can also do something for herself. She can stop using her husband as an excuse to slip into egoistic resentment and violence.

Both husband and wife need a basic and effective solution to their problems. The solution is God. It is all summed up in these words: "Set your mind on God's kingdom and his justice before everything else, and all the rest will come to you as well" (Matt. 6:33 NEB).

3. *The Individual in Relation to His Children.*

91

We have already seen that the person whose life-style is basically ego-centered is a troubled, problem-laden individual. When this person brings children into the world, he fashions them into his own image. He also worships them as he worships himself, for his god is man.

From Adam and Eve on down to today, human parents train their children to sin their sins. The mother whose goddishness is expressed by an overprotective, perfectionistic training of her child will see these very attitudes in full operation when the grandchild arrives. Note that at the time of such training, the mother's intent is to help the child and save him from costly errors. The mother feels anxious and insecure. Certainly the last thing she wishes to hear is that she is a god-player. But she is. Look at her damaged child. The child is a human sacrifice offered in worship to mother.

Mothers and fathers can do even worse things to their children, however, than to overdirect them. A much more destructive way of damaging children is to withhold discipline from them. The child is then permitted, we are told, to grow up naturally. After all, how will the child learn self-discipline if he is constantly inhibited by external parental discipline? Why restrain the basic goodness of a child?

The reason the parent withholds discipline from his child is because the *parent* wishes to live without discipline. We can hardly expect much else. The parent builds his philosophy of life into his task of child-rearing, and if the parent is ultimate—that is, under no higher authority, hence, not under God—then we can hardly expect him to impose a discipline upon his child, except possibly for some self-serving reasons.

It follows, too, that a parent who defaults in disciplining his child will rather concentrate on building his ego. The child is handed buckets of encouragement and praise, not to mention a number of well-chosen bribes which are dangled before him to activate his egoistic glands and muscles. The parents sincerely feel that their child has no problem with sin—that is, with god-playing. There is nothing wrong with the child. The child, we are told, simply needs love, praise, encouragement, and still more love, praise, and encouragement. The egocentric parents also want love, praise, and encouragement for their own lives, feeling that there is nothing wrong with themselves. They feel they are essentially lovable, worthy of praise, and headed in a direction in life which merits encouragement. As for god-playing, this does not register with them as a problem. So why should it be a problem to the child?

Eventually, such children become a terrible problem to themselves, not to mention a burden to others. When this happens, the current professional advice is to listen to the child. *Really* listen to him. And of course, no one denies that this is good, but if all we do is listen, it may do great harm. Mere listening may fortify the I-centeredness of the child. Just listening also encourages a person to further embed in his mind his sick feelings and faulty style of life. Of much more value than mere listening is for the child to be challenged, lovingly countered, invited to accept God's terms for his young life. This entails the death of the I-centeredness—a benefit which mere listening can never bring.

If listening is not enough, neither is keeping the child happy, enough for the training of the child. Most parents feel that a happy, secure childhood, free from any difficult deprivation, is the most important foundation in the child's life. It cannot be denied that this is important, but not so important as providing discipline and authority for the child.

We have some friends who are presently in the process of a divorce. They have children. Will the children be damaged by the divorce? Of course they will. They will receive less love. Yet the greatest danger in that situation is not the loss of love (because no child ever feels he gets enough of that anyway) but that with the severing of parental authority, the child will rush through the breach with only one parent (probably badly shaken from the divorce) around to stop him. *That* is how children from broken homes really get hurt.

My wife and I have some gifted friends who were childless for many years. They finally adopted two beautiful children—twins—and from that moment, smothered these children with nothing but love and affection. This was the way to insure that they would become normal, healthy adults, we were told. Today, the son is in prison, and the daughter has left home. Their poor parents still do not understand what went wrong. They tried so hard. They gave so much. But they seldom said *no* to them, never having realized that discipline is the highest form of love. Now the children hate the parents. There seems to be a law in the world which says that if authority-bearers default in the use of their authority, their children who are deprived of this blessing will rise up to destroy these "authorities."

Not too long ago, a middle-aged man whose god-playing parents had showered him with all kinds of permissiveness sat in my study. He was slightly intoxicated but sober enough to say, "My problem is that nobody has cared enough or had the guts to say *no* to me. I am surrounded by nice people who are afraid to counter me, afraid to tell me that I am a damn fool for doing what I intend to do. Oh, for somebody to cross me. That's what I need. That's why I've come."

I do not agree with a colleague who said that this man was simply working out his sick dependency needs on me. I feel that man was exactly on target as to what he needed. I was careful, however, not to give him exactly what he wanted. If I had shouted "No!" to him, he would have revolted in his typically egoistic fashion. But I did counter his whole life in offering him new terms, new discipline, new counsel which he was free to accept or reject.

Were my parishioner a young child and were I his father, I would have used some loving coercion on him. This is precisely what our mothers used on us during our toilet-training. We could fight mother and she would still love us, but it had to be *her* way. This is a good parent. Many parents wish they had used this principle with their children's piano lessons. After, say, a year, the child wants to quit. The parents foolishly say, "We leave it up to you." What they should say is, "No. We want you to continue. You once made a decision to play the piano, but regardless of your feelings, continue. Now you have a half hour of practicing to do yet."

Which all leads me in reflection to say that children need three basic things from parental authorities:

    a. Loving coercion.

    b. Loving limits to their behavior.

    c. Loving love, by which I mean a love free from possessiveness and filled with patience, warmth, and acceptance.

I am tempted to add a fourth point to the effect that children need parents who will love themselves when they fail to meet these goals perfectly.

The key to being a good parent, I am sure, lies in being solidly positioned in the Kingdom of God. Anyone under God's rule has settled the question of authority in his life, and now he can properly represent Authority to his children. Without God, parents are angrily authoritarian, which is the last thing a child needs. He needs loving, disciplining authority in his life.

Normally, a child will respond to authority with obedience. Those who insist that obedience damages the natural spontaneity of a child lead us astray. We know better, even from our experience with dogs. We all understand that a dog needs training. Without discipline, a dog grows up wild, hating himself and others. Dogs enjoy their lives when they are well-trained and disciplined. Would that we thought as much of our children as we do of our dogs! There is a way to stop raising trained dogs but wild children.

The way is God.

4. *The Individual in Relation to His Authority-Bearers.*

God alone *is* Authority. But people do represent Him.

In the eyes of the egocentric person, Authority, as well as His authority-bearers, are the enemies of his life. These "enemies"—parents, teachers, employers, policemen, judges, pastors, doctors, lawmakers, and so on—are a constant threat to his position as Number One in the world. The egoist resists the imposition of external authority upon his life. God and His surrogate authorities are experienced as dangerous intruders bent on the egoist's destruction. "God hates me," reported one man who told me in detail how he spent sixty years of his life under his own authority.

The I-centered person, in a word, wants to run his own show without any outsiders messing things up. He wants to be self-controlled. He calls that self-discipline. He has childlike faith in his childlike self. He believes with all his little heart in his I-will-power.

This self-discipline enslaves us. My friends in Alcoholics Anonymous tell me that practicing alcoholics *are* self-disciplined. They are living under the discipline of the Big I with all the willpower that is in them. When a person abandons will-powered self-discipline and gets under Higher Power, he becomes a free man. As one member put it bluntly, "I tried self-discipline with my alcoholism and my diarrhea. My approach had no noticeable effect in stopping either problem."

Self-discipline keeps us slaves to ourselves in the Kingdom of I. I want now to sketch how coming under authority-bearers tends to free us as persons. Following this, we will see that for one to really become free indeed, he will need to deal with Authority Himself. Two brief examples now of the liberation we experience when we submit to authority-bearers.

Think of the adolescent person. Recall how he resists

his parents when they set limits for him. The normal adolescent has episodes in which he kicks against, fights, vilifies, and not infrequently hurts his parents. Most of us parents are both stunned and frightened by what we see happening in our child. "How can this be in one who was such a beautiful baby and well-mannered boy?"

If, at this point, the parent resigns as a parent, as so many today do, we know what will happen to the child. Without the restraints of parental discipline, the child will fall apart. It is almost as if he shakes himself to pieces because there is no hand to steady him.

Hopefully, the parent will retain his role as parent, continuing to hold his position of authority with a firm, loving hand. Almost invariably, as the period passes, the child will come to terms with the parent and be the more mature because of it. When the parental authority-bearer patiently does his job, he is really laying a solid foundation in the child's life so that the child can become free. Free from whom? Free from himself.

A second illustration of freedom through discipline is found in patients who come voluntarily for treatment to a mental hospital. Today the major reasons for entering a mental hospital are: (1) an uncontrollable addiction; (2) attempted suicide or homicide; (3) other kinds of irresistible compulsions; (4) depression. When a person with any of these problems voluntarily admits himself to a hospital, almost without fail he is amazed to find that his symptoms almost disappear after a week or ten days. The change is almost miraculous. Hard-core drug addicts often report that they no longer desire heroin. The moment they leave, however, the addiction returns full-force.

Not too long ago, two of my alcoholic parishioners discovered some vodka which a thoughtless visitor had left under a tree on the grounds of the hospital.

"Here was this bottle of Smirnoff's staring us right in the face. Would you believe us, Chaplain, that neither of us even wanted a drink of it? We could have drunk it and gotten away with it (because vodka leaves no odor on the breath), but we decided to turn it in to the ward nurse."

I was glad with these men for their victory over alcohol. Their voluntary submission to God's authority as represented by the hospital, gave them this freedom.

More is needed for real freedom, however, than mere submission to an authority-bearer such as a hospital. One must go on to voluntary submission to God if one is to receive lasting freedom. "If the Son makes you free, you will be free indeed" (John 8:36).

Sad to say, one of these men began drinking soon after leaving the discipline of our hospital. Without the hospital and a central place for God in his life, he became his own authority—with the inevitable results.

All this leads me to state in a sentence the main thesis of this chapter: We are to be subject to no man but God—yet we are to be subject unto God through human authority-bearers. My point is simply that submission to God without the mediation of authority-bearers is often just another way of talking to ourselves, because in that private dialogue between God and the soul, we can often get God to say most anything we want Him to say. On the other hand, submission to authority-bearers without submission to God is a return to the worship of man. Inseparably join the two—submission to God and authority-bearers—and we are in the Kingdom of God. This kind of obedience brings us authentically and realistically under God's control.

Most people, I find, think that submission to God is all that is required. It is sufficient, several have pointed out to me, just to deal with God. I once believed this myself and even recommended it from a pulpit. These were the days when I neither sought nor felt I needed the counsel of fellow Christians. After all, why consult with them when I could talk directly with God?

I'd like to answer that question. Why consult the advice of a brother in Christ? Because, quite honestly.

too often I cannot tell the difference between the voice of God and the voice of my own egoism. Too many times I have claimed to be following the will of God when everyone around me knew perfectly well I was following the will of Earl. Had I only turned to a brother or sister in Christ and asked for his impartial counsel and then accepted it, I would have avoided a rendezvous with my own folly.

A brother in Christ as a spiritual adviser is now someone without whom I cannot live. It has gotten through to me that God can never be separated from His people. There is a triangle in my life composed of God, another theocentric person, and myself as a theocentric person—

The linear relationship between God and myself is surely basic and needful, but the triangular relationship is even more needful, because it corrects what I hear God saying to me in the linear. God speaks to me through my brother in Christ. My spiritual adviser is the primary bearer of God's authority into my life, I see God in him. I hear the voice of God through my adviser.

"I envy you," someone might say, "with such a wonderful spiritual adviser in your life. Such a strong person! So wise, too! I just don't have any people like that in my life. Too bad for me."

Would you allow me, my friend, to be your spiritual

adviser for a few minutes? I have something to say on behalf of the Lord we both serve.

What I hear from my spiritual adviser is frequently something I don't want to hear. At times he will cross my will and then just patiently stand there until I have the humility to become obedient. Sometimes it takes me a month to raise all my objections and play out the procrastination game before I get around to doing what is suggested. The rule I now follow is that unless my Christ-representative's advice is clearly contrary to the Word of God and my conscience, I will just do it. Do it out of obedience to God. I don't have to like His will—I just have to do it.

I disagree with you—flatly and completely. I don't agree that my spiritual adviser is a special breed of spiritual giant. Neither would he, incidentally, agree with you. In addition, we both feel that God has a spiritual adviser for every one of His people, yourself included.

You have an image in your mind of a spiritual adviser who would have the wisdom of Solomon, the patience of Job, and the brilliance of Paul. There is no such person—not in your life, nor in mine. My spiritual adviser is a very ordinary Christian with ordinary talents. He does possess, however, one virtue which fully qualifies him for his role: God has given him a genuine humility—a demonstrable humility—which is proven by the fact that he has chosen to place *himself* under a spiritual adviser. It is the fact that he is verifiably under submission to Christ through his spiritual adviser, that qualifies him to be one to me.

"But I *still* don't see that kind of a person in my life," you respond.

It may be true—but it need not be. Why would it not be possible for you to approach a Christian friend and have an agreement that you would cross-advise each other? Why could you not meet regularly to share your lives and seek the Lord's will through each other's prayers and advice? Would that not place you both under the authority of Christ in a tangible way?

"Should not such a person be a pastor?" He may be, but not necessarily. Look only for someone who knows Christ and is led by the Holy Spirit.

"What if he gives me the *wrong* advice?" Do nothing against your conscience—but everything against your willfulness. Begin with those issues where you can both agree that the advice is the will of God.

As your temporary spiritual adviser, I have a suggestion to make: Ask God for such a person in your life. Here is a prayer you can use:

Heavenly Father, I now understand that I need a spiritual adviser in this relationship with You. Lead me to the person You have in mind for me. Reveal the person's name to me. And once I know this person, give me the freedom to speak up and share my need. You be the power for all this—both in me to ask, and in the other person to accept. I believe that my prayer has already been answered. In the Name of Jesus, Amen.

There are other people besides spiritual advisers who represent Christ to us. Indeed, we should see Christ in our employers, in the local policemen, in ecclesiastical courts, in government officials, in the law of the land, etc. We can affirm the words of Peter in the New Testament as consummate wisdom:

Be subject for the Lord's sake to every human institution, whether it be to the emperor as supreme, or to governors as sent by him to punish those who do wrong and to praise those who do right. (I Pet. 2:13-14)

Paul says the same thing:

Let every person be subject to the governing authorities. For there is no authority except from God, and those that exist have been instituted by God. Therefore he who resists the authorities resists what God has appointed. (Rom. 13:1-2)

Slaves, be obedient to those who are your earthly
masters, with fear and trembling, in singleness of
heart, as to Christ . . . doing the will of God from
the heart. (Eph. 6:5-6)

"But how far does this obedience go?" someone
asks. "Does one blindly obey a corrupt law? And when
the authority-bearer is obviously in error, what are we
to do—support him in his folly?" Two examples:

A twelve-year-old boy was in great distress when his
father said to him, "You *must* pass this exam. If you
must cheat to pass it, cheat. Just don't get caught. But
you must pass the exam." What counsel would you
give such a boy?

A friend of mine who is in business asked me, "My
employer insists that I falsify some figures in an important report. I run the risk of being fired if I do not
cooperate. What should I do?"

These are tough questions, so we must brace ourselves for some demanding answers.

We are to obey authority-bearers only insofar as they
conform to the law of God. When human authority is
in conflict with God's authority—and we may need
spiritual counsel from other people in the Kingdom of
God to know when that point is reached—it seems to
me that we have no alternative but to disobey. We are
to transcend human authority and be subject to God
alone at such a time.

I don't know whether my brief explanation in the
preceding paragraph satisfies you or not. I know it
would not satisfy my parishioners, who are mental
patients. Such a person would probably say to me,
"So what do I *do*? How do I handle such a situation?
Okay—you've give me the general principle but how do
I apply it?"

I would suggest three concrete actions.

a. *Love the disobedient authority-bearers.* Our first
duty is to look to ourselves rather than immediately to
the sins of others. The need for this action is very

great, because faults in the authority-bearer have a way of drawing out our egotism. His sins evoke in us judgment, haughtiness, self-righteousness, anger, violence, etc.

It is so important, therefore, to love the "enemy"— the more so when he is undeniably wrong. It is our task to correct our attitude toward him and express to him Christ's love through us, both in friendly words and selfless deeds.

b. *Pray for the disobedient authority-bearer.* He sorely needs your prayers. Ask God to lead him away from sin. Pray that the Holy Spirit will give him a change of heart so that he will abandon his wicked plans. Draw upon the limitless power of God to change the "impossibles" in this conflict.

c. *React non-violently.* This means that we refuse to comply with what is unlawfully demanded of us. Indeed, it is our duty to violate corrupt laws and attempt to substitute just laws in their place.

A classic model of non-violent reaction is found in the early Church soon after Pentecost. The religious authorities "arrested the apostles and put them in the common prison. But at night an angel of the Lord opened the prison doors and brought them out and said, 'Go and stand in the temple and speak to the people all the words of this Life'" (Acts 5:18-20). The apostles did as the angel commanded until once again they were arrested and brought before the Council. Peter bluntly told them, "We must obey God rather than men" (v. 29). After beating the apostles, the Council charged them not to speak in the name of Jesus. But they did. "And every day in the temple and at home, they did not cease teaching and preaching Jesus as the Christ" (v. 42).

It is difficult, as we all know, to know just when to resist and when to comply. Sometimes we are awake all night trying to figure out where to draw the line in our lives between the lawful and unlawful. We search and investigate until we are weary, trying to determine whether a given authority-representative is under the law or above it.

These difficult choices clearly illustrate the need for a spiritual adviser in our lives. God will use such a person to free us from an ego-biased decision. Understand, of course, that we do not ask the spiritual adviser to make our decisions. The spiritual adviser is vested with advisory power—not the power of decision. Each person is responsible before his Lord for his own decisions.

It is true, also, that God can and does speak directly to a person through the Holy Spirit. When we are brought before governors and kings, we are not to be anxious about what we are to say, for the Holy Spirit will tell us what to speak (Mark 13:11). The Holy Spirit is speaking directly to the hearts of His people today as never before, praise the Lord. By conferring with a spiritual adviser, however, as to the content of the Holy Spirit's revelation to us, we have a sure way to confirm that it is indeed the Holy Spirit speaking to us, rather than our human spirits or evil spirits.

What is really at issue here, is whether one is ready to hear the truth about himself. The Holy Spirit is the spirit of truth. We should be so willing to hear His truth that we would not be at all concerned about the quarter from which it is coming. Ideally, the Spirit's truth should be welcomed from any person who calls Jesus, Lord. Because of our spiritual weakness, this kind of openness to the truth may be too intense for us.

So we begin, therefore, with one person, whom I have been calling a spiritual adviser. We ask him to tell us the truth about ourselves.

This is the beginning of what the Bible calls "living in the light."

Let us now go on to look at two ways which claim to bring us into the light but do not They are egocentric religion and humanistic psychology.

7

Man's Way of Attempting to Enter
the Kingdom of God

1. The Pseudo-Religious Approach.

Do you recall Rob, of whom I spoke in Chapter One? I described his early life as an aspiring ball-player and his suicidal problem in later life. Rob is an example of a person who attempted to use a pseudo-religious approach to his life-problems. This worsened his problems. But let Rob tell you about it:

I always came away from this minister feeling that I had to do more than I was doing. God knows, I was trying my best, but still more was asked of me. I was told that I had to get ahold of myself and use some willpower. This pastor talked a great deal about finding my own answers and needing to grow up. Well, I knew that before I came to him. Fact is, I *had* no answers and didn't know *how* to grow up. That's why I came to him. When this minister also gave me some books to read, I almost felt like saying, "Don't I have enough burdens?"

The pastor soon got me involved in his church. I began attending a class in Old Testament history. Also attended church quite often and began reading the Bible rather regularly—the whole bit. The pastor assured me that if I prayed every day, God would help me fight these suicidal feelings. Well, I was hoping that this minister would pray with me, but he never suggested it. So I prayed alone. But I could feel that I was losing interest.

I suppressed my feelings of sadness as Rob talked. Here was yet another needy person who had come to a minister who could not minister to the person's real needs. Rob needed God. The pastor gave him a program of religious activity. And it was all such *good* activity! Only none of it brought Rob the immediate kind of salvation he needed.

Rob's pastor offered him four different kinds of religious activity: the acquisition of religious knowledge and a belief in it, the exercise of self-denial and the use of willpower, the use of petitionary prayer, and the habit of worship. Would you agree that this is fairly typical of what Rob might be offered in the vast majority of our churches? Hundreds of patients have told me that this is what they get from their pastors. And it doesn't work, they tell me. And I agree with them. Salvation by religious activity never delivers us from our bondages, clerical claims to the contrary notwithstanding.

Let us look a little more closely at each of the four kinds of religious activity mentioned above.

a. *The acquisition of religious knowledge and a belief in it.* In the case of Rob, religious knowledge referred to knowledge about the Bible and the church. Few ministers would argue about the need for such knowledge, but most ministers today feel that we need much more than mere Bible knowledge. Specifically, we need psychological knowledge. My impression is that most ministers believe in psychology about as much as they believe in the Bible. This produces a counseling pastor who tries to blend the two kinds of knowledge together in order to fit the needs of the parishioner.

The psychologist-pastor now begins to use his knowledge on people. He delves into the past history of his client to find out how the problem began. The pastor tries to explain the intricate workings of the interpersonal games which the counselee is playing and which others are playing on him. The minister sometimes explains, sometimes confronts, and sometimes hits his parishioner on the head with something called "reality." If the thick-skulled parishioner is stubbornly unteachable, he is invariably referred to someone who possesses a great deal more knowledge. He is the psychiatrist—awesome idol of all aspiring pastoral counselors.

But now, what about the acquisition of some good psychologically enlightened religious knowledge? Is that not the medicine which the sick parishioner needs?

I feel it is not.

The acquisition of more knowledge and understanding presupposes our competence to save ourselves, even if only in some small way. Feed the presupposition that we can help ourselves through a little additional knowledge, and you will find no needful place for God in our problems. After all, if we ourselves can do it, who needs Him?

In my experience, people with problems are helped only minimally with psychologically tinged religious knowledge. We never were, nor will we ever be, delivered from the bondages of sin by human knowledge. Therefore, we should abandon this dead-end street and turn to the Way who is Jesus Christ.

b. *The exercise of self-denial and the use of will-power.* The best that Rob's pastor could muster was the advice to stop entertaining those thoughts about suicide and to begin to get ahold of himself by means of willpower.

Such is not the message of Christ. He never told us we could do anything (in our own strength) if we only really tried. Christ never used His time preaching sermons to provoke people into making one additional, herculean effort to put them on top of their problems.

"It's up to you!" So many clergymen conclude their counsel with this rejective falsehood. I confess that there was a stage in my own ministry when I was sure my best help was to force the parishioner to take responsibility for his life and *do* something with it. Filled with a sense of omnipotence myself, I urged this upon others.

"Yes," says the helpless parishioner, "I guess God helps those who help themselves, just like the Bible says." Nowhere in the Bible do these words, or anything like them, appear.

Salvation by the grace of God rather than hard work is the most basic teaching of the Bible. And since nothing has really changed in the human heart since biblical times, it remains the central issue in our lives today. Any counsel which is offered on behalf of the Church of Jesus Christ ought to recognize that we are saved by grace alone. Our technique of pastoral counseling should be based on that premise. When it is, the power of God moves in to save mightily.

c. *The use of petitionary prayer.* "Say a little prayer for me, Chaplain." I can count on someone saying this to me at least once a day as I pass through the hospital wards. I have two responses to the request.

If the request is from a patient whom I do not know very well, I'll stop to ask, "For what would you like me to pray?" When the inquirer sufficiently recovers his composure, he usually tells me about his broken arm, or his empty bank account, or his wife who is having a baby.

There are other patients whom I know very well. In

response to their request for a little prayer, I some-times good-naturedly say, "In your case, it will take more than a *little* prayer—and if you've got a minute, I'd like to talk with you about something you need be-fore we begin praying. So let's sit down and talk about it."

I am not quick, you notice, to offer prayers for God's help. For if the person requesting prayer is an egocen-tric, he is offering the wrong prayer. Egoists should not be encouraged to ask God for help, for a number of reasons.

The cry for help is not the prayer God is waiting to hear. He is waiting to hear our word of obedient sur-render. God wants only one thing from us—our wills, subordinate to His will. No humanitarian service, no worship, no prayer means anything until the issue of our wills is settled. We ought to give Him what *He* wants, not what *we* want.

The cry of the egoist for help is essentially foxhole religion: "God, I'm in real trouble. Get me out of this trouble so that I can continue on my old self-centered way." Because of God's mercy, the prayer is oftentimes answered, but how long will God indulge us?

There is a vast difference between praying, "God, help me to get things under control again," and pray-ing, "Lord, You take over. It has gotten to a point where only Your divine power can help this situation. I'll follow You out of this problem." In the first prayer, God is asked to be a copilot. In the second, the Pilot.

I began my work as a mental hospital chaplain pray-ing that God would go with me on the wards and help me to do my work. I was the pilot, and God was my co-pilot. It is completely different now. I now understand that God is on the wards long before I get there. God does not arrive at 8:30 A.M. when I enter the ward. He has been working in my people for years. When I step on the ward, I am privileged to enter into His work, and anything that happens to the patients is a result of

His power. How different, easier, and better. God is the Pilot. I am a copilot.

d. *The habit of worship.* The whole idea of worship, if I understand it correctly, is that it be a response to the saving grace of God. Unfortunately, worship can be engaged in for any number of reasons. Today a woman told me that she regularly went to worship on Sunday morning before spending the evening in a motel with another woman's husband. When I asked whether this created any conflict in her mind, she said, "Sometimes, but it would not be right if I didn't spend part of the day with God." You notice how carefully my parishioner guards her claim to righteousness.

Granted, my example is a little extreme, but it does reflect an attitude among all too many of us that worship is what God really wants from us. Going to church comes to be the essential thing. Most pastors, sad to say, are perfectly content with their parishioners as long as they keep worshiping. As the cleric looks over the worshipers on Sunday morning, he is not concerned about *why* they are there. *That* they are present is enough.

But mere attendance does not please the Lord. God looks at the heart of the worshiper to see if there is obedience. "Has the Lord as great delight in burnt offerings and sacrifice, as in obeying the voice of the Lord? Behold, to obey is better than sacrifice, and to hearken than the fat of rams" (I Sam. 15:22). Worship which is not preceded by an obedient relationship to Jesus Christ is mere empty ritual.

I'll take that back. It is not *empty* ritual, for ritual can be filled with egoism. That kind of ritual thrives on saying things right, looking right, feeling right. The egocentric mind is attracted to this futile, endless exercise in perfectionism.

In summary, the worship of God should not be used as a means of straightening out our troubled lives. Such worship is merely a meaningless ritual which is as burdensome to the worshiper as to God.

"What's wrong," one may ask, "with this advice from the pastor? Isn't it a good thing to enlarge our knowledge, use our willpower, say our prayers, and attend worship? Seems to me this ought to help a little bit. Maybe it will lead to better things."

Nonsense! The whole approach is unworthy of a suffering person. We do not find God by taking little bits and pieces of religious activity into our troubled lives. When a person has a skin cancer, it is not enough to take some vitamins, cover it with ointment, expose it to the sun, and later keep it carefully bandaged. What is needed is surgery. Anything else is the wrong treatment for skin cancer. All efforts at do-it-yourself treatment must cease. One must surrender himself into the hands of a good surgeon.

It was the same with Rob. He did not need religion. He needed God. What his pastor should have done, was bring Rob to God. Rob needed to surrender himself to Jesus Christ as Lord. This is the first step. Nothing really can be done for any of our problems until that issue has been decided. The issue is God.

Rob's pastor could have said, "You've told me a lot about your problems. I know you have tried everything, but nothing seems to work—your life is still unmanageable. But you may be ready for something better, Rob. I can offer you a choice. You can either continue as your own manager and struggle on with your problems, or you can ask Jesus Christ to become the manager of your life. Do you feel ready to come to a decision on this matter today?"

We certainly understand and accept the fact that the pastor who advises salvation through a program of religious activity sincerely means well. I am sure, too, that there is much love behind the counsel he offers. But what is lacking in such a man is a surrendered and obedient heart. Not possessing this himself, he will not suggest the need for it to others. Such is the sad and tragic state of affairs today with the vast majority of Christian clergymen.

What can be done? What can possibly be done about all these clergymen today who lead people to pseudo-religion rather than to God?

"There is a way," claims a famous seminary in a recent issue of *Christianity Today*. The advertisement promises to "give you a knowledge and working plan to solve the problems of Modern Man." All one needs to do is attend that seminary. Indeed, most modern Christianity has committed itself to a doctrine of salvation for the church through seminary training.

Older pastors are placed under pressure to obtain continuing education in our seminaries. "Today's minister must cope with the congregation's changing values, life-styles, problems, and attitudes. He may need knowledge and skills which were not even available when he completed his formal education. This is why his continuing education is so vitally important."

Would that, perhaps, not help?

No, the seminaries have not yet saved that large company of ministers who cannot minister. It is doubtful that they ever will.

"The only thing to do," cries a layman, "is to get rid of the deadwood! It's time to take a whip and clean out the temple. Any ordained minister who can't preach the Word of God should be barred from the pulpit!"

The Christian church has been conducting heresy trials all its long life. I can give you examples of churches which have totally preoccupied themselves with keeping themselves pure, but the heretics continue to multiply.

Is there not some way, some reasonable approach, which can free us from the yoke of clerical bondage?

I, truthfully, do not know of any way.

I believe the situation is quite beyond us. All our strategies to redeem and remedy the pastoral leadership of the church have failed. We are in the position—if we can only admit it—of an alcoholic who has hit bottom and has no more plans, no more excuses, no more ideas. We have tried everything, and there is nothing left to do. Our egoism and sin have driven us into an impossible position.

Impossible, that is, with men.

Not God.

We in the church have tried everything except giving up. It is time to surrender to God both ourselves and our problem. If the shepherds and their sheep are to be saved—and I believe they *will* be saved—God will have to do it.

Our hope is in the Lord alone, not in man.

As I close this section, I must share with you the deep feelings of joy and hope in my heart at this moment. Do not be frightened or angered by the disorder in our Lord's church. Thank God, our destiny does not rest upon what we have or have not done! Our hope is not in human strength, but in God.

And I want you to know that God's plans for His Church are coming along beautifully. He knows where He is going with us. We are in good hands. The best is yet to come. Neither the powers of hell, nor even our own shortcomings, will prevail against Christ's Church.

So rejoice and be filled with hope.

Catch the vision of Isaiah, who lived at a time when things looked very dark. The nation of Israel, already divided, would soon go into captivity and become dispersed. But Isaiah is filled with faith and love as he says:

Remember not the former things,
 nor consider the things of old.
Behold, I am doing a new thing;
 now it springs forth, do you not perceive it?
I will make a way in the wilderness
 and rivers in the desert. (43:18-19)

2. *The Psychological Approach*

Let me tell you about my life a dozen years ago.

I was at that time a frustrated parish pastor who was ready to get out of the ministry. Not having the courage to make the break, I decided to do what many confused clergymen do—I began to take a postgraduate course called "clinical training." The field was pastoral psychology, and this suited me well because it was 98 percent psychology and 2 percent religion.

The dark night of my soul in the parish was ended by the bright morning light of Sigmund Freud and the lesser luminaries who followed him. Psychiatry gave me *answers*—and techniques—and a whole new understanding of myself and my world. It was intoxicating and, I felt, a vast improvement over what I had. With the enthusiasm of a new convert, I went into psychotherapy with a strong desire to work out my emotional salvation. My commitment to the science of the mind was enthusiastic, strong, and expectant. I was fascinated by what psychiatry and psychology promised us in the way of maturation, emotional health, interpersonal growth, *et cetera* and *ad infinitum*. Any pain I endured in therapy or in training was not to be compared to the joys of finding my true Self (a word which I soon found myself capitalizing along with other terms of deity).

Perhaps you will be reassured to hear that I did not follow Sigmund Freud in his conviction that God was a projection of my father image. No, I would never say that. I kept God as a worthy religious term and as a rather good idea, but the only real function I saw for Him was to keep the world running smoothly while I worked myself out of my problems. God's function was to keep me strong and in good shape. For this cooperation, I piously thanked Him, but I was not ready at this stage in my life to make room for His authority and power over me. I honestly thought I was doing quite nicely all by myself. My psychiatric colleagues supported my delusion.

It came time to enter the mental hospital chaplaincy

work for which I had been duly trained. Looking back, I see that I should have entered as a patient rather than a chaplain, because I soon found myself in real distress in at least two ways.

Increasingly, I could not stand myself. Clinical training and psychotherapy, though at first I was intrigued and dazzled by their results, left me morbidly introspective and still groping for answers to life. A cloud of depression hung over me.

Externally, I was doing just fine. I'm sure that my friends were unaware of my growing despair, but it was there. A person can usually hide his wounds from his friends, but when the friends are away and the person alone, what suffering it is to stare at the wounds and admit that the "surgery" has brought no healing.

The second kind of distress I encountered was in my ministry to the emotionally ill who came to the hospital for treatment. I already knew that sermons, Bible reading, and praying were not setting the prisoners free from their neurotic and addictive prisons. What I soon came to realize was that group therapy, chemotherapy, analytic theory, and the therapeutic community were not doing it, either. For a brief period, I tried frantically to combine the best of both psychiatry and religion, but to no avail. Neither discipline measurably affected my people. In fact, there was mounting evidence that they would actually heal faster if we just left them alone on the wards.*

A case in point was a man whom we'll call Milton. The hospital staff all agreed that this well-educated man was a highly motivated patient. He freely spoke to me of his past life and seemed to arrive at a whole series of helpful insights about himself. Other patients began to notice the change in Milton. He freely admitted, "I'm beginning to find out who I really am—

---

*The spontaneous remission rate for people admitted to mental hospitals and given only custodial care is 70 percent within eighteen months. This is higher than the percentages usually given for patients who have received various kinds of therapies.

and who I can become." I worked with Milton at a time when I was swept up in the newest psychological emphases on human potential, behavioral modification, and emotional catharsis.

Milton was released and did well for about three weeks but then had to return to the hospital. He was in worse condition than previously. He has since been discharged again. When he left, I remember suppressing my feeling that I had somehow failed terribly with this man.

I was about to resign as a chaplain and get into something useful like bricklaying or plumbing, when God turned my attention to an odd group of people whom I had always written off as superficial and somewhat naïve. In fact, during the first year of my ministry, I wrote a paper against them. They were the recovering alcoholics in Alcoholics Anonymous. As I suspiciously studied them, I suddenly began to realize that these people had what I was looking for! They were *new* people. Their whole style of life was changed. And they were quiet inside—something they called serenity. They were also joyful. Best of all, they were *free*—free from their alcoholic prisons and a number of other prisons besides!

Their growing freedom did not please me. Like the elder brother in the parable of the Prodigal Son, I began to feel anger and jealousy toward my alcoholic brothers and sisters. I had always been watchful of my conduct and faithful to my calling as a minister. My money was wisely spent, and my family did not find themselves receiving government welfare checks. All through the years, I had faithfully served God—but for what? I, the faithful servant, was now the fool—and the real fools were rewarded! Even worse, I felt that God had duped me.

At the time, the whole experience registered with me as an absurd and senseless humiliation. It never occurred to me that this was about the only way possible for God to humble my pride. My damaged ego further intensified my need for an answer. Reluctantly, I admitted that these people in AA had what I needed.

So I began to sit at their feet and learn from them. Imagine me, with my degrees and ordination, learning the abc's of life from some broken people, many of whom had gone neither to school nor to church!

These dear people, however, knew God, and they began to talk to me about Him as a Higher Power who was *alive* and as One to whom we could give authority over our lives.

Suddenly I realized my folly. I had plenty of religion and plenty of psychiatry, but I had no God.

I surrendered my life to God.

My friends in AA helped me through the twelve steps* of their program. These steps work. I found out, not only with alcoholics but even with crazy, mixed-up ministers. God became real to me for the first time in my life. And so, ten years after my ordination, I stumbled into the Kingdom of God.

The lights began to go on. I heard music. I danced, not with my feet but in my heart. An answer had come into my life, and the Answer was not an idea, nor an insight, nor a method—but a Person.

When He entered my life, I immediately knew Him. He was Jesus Christ.

*The twelve steps are as follows: (1) We admitted we were powerless over alcohol — that our lives had become unmanageable. (2) Came to believe that a Power greater than ourselves could restore us to sanity. (3) Made a decision to turn our will and our lives over to the care of God as we understood Him. (4) Made a searching and fearless moral inventory of ourselves. (5) Admitted to God, to ourselves, and to another human being the exact nature of our wrongs. (6) Were entirely ready to have God remove all these defects of character. (7) Humbly asked Him to remove our shortcomings. (8) Made a list of all persons we had harmed, and became willing to make amends to them all. (9) Made direct amends to such people wherever possible, except when to do so would injure them or others. (10) Continued to take personal inventory, and when we were wrong, promptly admitted it. (11) Sought through prayer and meditation to improve our conscious contact with God as we understood Him, praying only for knowledge of His will for us and the power to carry that out. (12) Having had a spiritual awakening as the result of these steps, we tried to carry this message to alcoholics, and to practice these principles in all our affairs. (Used by permission)

Things have not been the same since.

Not with me nor with my patients. I've made a list of some of our new understandings. You will understand that they are not really new. Actually, all we do is rediscover the ancient truths of God which He has long been revealing to His people.

a. The basic problem with man is not that he is an immature child but rather that he is an egocentric godplayer.

Granted, we *feel* the opposite. We feel small, victimized, weak. But we *act* like gods, which is easily proven when we remember how we have judged and punished others; how we have tried to do the work of two or three people; how we have bucked authority right up the line. Man, in relation to Authority, tries to displace Him, compete with Him, forget Him, even destroy Him. Each of us wants, as we saw earlier, to be ultimate from childhood on. And all the while, we feel small and call ourselves immature.

So long as a person can be seen as immature, so long will we see him as innocent and sinless. After all, in our eyes, it is no sin to be immature. We might then be called weak, but surely not sinful. The next step in this kind of thinking, after claiming personal righteousness for oneself, is to accuse Authority (God) and His authority-representatives of being the sinners.

Does that really happen? Of course it does. The most constant themes in psychological literature are the evil effect of parents upon their children and the evil effect of institutions (with their repressive laws) upon adults. If parents and institutions can be faulted for one's problems, the individual is relieved of all responsibility and, therefore, of his sin and its ever-accompanying burden of guilt.

I no longer buy that.

I've gone back to the ancient answer: I myself am a sinner.

And, let me add, a strong sinner—willful, adamant, unbending. This is an accurate description of us all in our emotional illnesses. We are not weak people as far as our wills are concerned. Our feelings may be raw, our minds may be playing strange tricks on us, and our nervous systems may be overloaded, but our wills are as strong as iron and set in the firm concrete of our egocentric lives.

If it is true that the basic problem is sin rather than immaturity, then it also follows that the problem is basically spiritual rather than psychological. My recovering alcoholic friends were the first to point out to me that alcoholism is basically a spiritual problem —but not a religious problem. They frankly told me that what they needed was not more religion. They said they were engaged in the practice of spirituality and that they had found God. A half-million sober alcoholics, I decided, was too formidable a group to refute.

b. The basic answer to life's problems has been revealed.

The Answer is God.

I no longer agree with my brothers who look for the answers to life in endless research projects. The answer has been found. We did not find it. The Answer came to us, not we to the Answer. In a real sense, we can now stop looking.

The Answer, obviously, was never in man in the first place.

A sentence in the Old Testament speaks directly to my heart on this point. "The fear of the Lord is the beginning of wisdom, and knowledge of the Holy One is insight" (Prov. 9:10). Answers to life come when we finally get straight in our hearts who is Lord of our lives. If I am lord, then all the answers will have to be found in me. This is the path of self-realization. If God in Jesus Christ is Lord, then the answers are in Him. This means that I can stop my frantic, fruitless search, because the Answer has arrived.

Psychiatry and psychology (and religion) can never be accused of laziness in searching for answers. In the field of psychiatry alone last year, over 100,000 learned articles were published. This does not include thousands of technical books, not to mention hundreds of conferences where various speakers told about "Recent Developments in the Field of You Name It." Characteristically, these scholars disdain the accomplishments of the past, as they disclose to us the newest discoveries which, we are assured, constitute a revolutionary breakthrough to the understanding of ourselves.

I no longer believe that.

My faith in man is too weak. I am a man of little faith in man. One must have a deep faith and an abiding trust to accept all these recent developments which will be replaced next year by even newer discoveries. I wish I had such faith! It is not easy to be an unbeliever these days.

It seems to be one of God's odd quirks that throughout human history, He keeps on displaying the folly of human knowledge and wisdom when they are godless. This is because the answer to life is not something we can put into propositional form. The answer to our tangled, troubled lives is a Person. He is God.

Listen to what Paul wrote to the Christians at Corinth, some nineteen centuries ago:

Not many of you were wise according to worldly standards, not many were powerful, not many were of noble birth; but God chose what is foolish in the world to shame the wise, God chose what is weak in the world to shame the strong, God chose what is low and despised in the world, even things that are not, to bring to nothing things that are, so that no human being might boast in the presence of God. He is the source of your life in Christ Jesus, whom God made our wisdom, our righteousness and sanctification and redemption. (I Cor. 1:26-30)

That, I believe.

If this understanding is correct, then a number of

things seem to follow for those of us who are professionally involved in counseling:

a. The most fatal mistake in counseling is made when the counselor begins with an assumption of his omnipotence.

b. God can no longer be deliberately excluded from the counseling process.

c. Counseling, if it is to have any deep and lasting effect, must include the suggestion to confess our sins and the suggestion to surrender the self to God.

d. The day of the professional counselor may soon be finished.

Let us consider each point:

a. The most fatal mistake in counseling is made when the counselor begins with an assumption of his omnipotence.

When a humanistically oriented behavioral scientist sits down with a patient, I believe he makes his greatest mistake even before he opens his mouth. He does this by assuming a closed system in which all the factors are enclosed within the relationship between the healer and the sick person. Since it is the expectation that the healer do some healing, he begins to apply his skills and effort upon the sick person. In the world of modern counseling, it is seldom that a healer questions his ability to comprehend the problem and solve it by means of his professional skill. If results are not forthcoming, the sick person is said to be unco operative, or unmotivated, or unable to benefit from treatment. Very rarely does the counselor question his quiet assumption of omniscience and omnipotence.

There is no place for God in such a system.

At most, God is sometimes asked to assist the healing process, but the process itself is thought to be the healing agent. Healing is supposed to take place through the therapeutic relationship set up by the healer. Everything depends upon the efforts and expertise of the healer to set this up.

I can no longer go along with such an understanding.

The most I can basically do for another human being is: help him discern that his painful bondage is the fruit of his egocentric life-style; ask him if he is ready to leave his egocentric world in order to enter the Kingdom of God; and suggest some concrete acts and steps by which he can make concrete his obedience to God. Note that the power to move a person to such action will need to be God. I only place things on the table. If anyone picks up what I have placed on the table, it is because of God's power, not mine. God has *all* power, especially in counseling work.

But should we not use both approaches—a full use of man's power and a full use of God's power? No—no more than we should move our cars, to use an illustration, by the engine and the starter at the same time. The car will move on one or the other—not both. A similar law applies to God and man. The Scriptures teach that we are saved by God alone without man's work. Salvation, whether in this world or in the next, is a work of God. All we can do is accept it. We cannot earn it.

Yet is not human help oftentimes effective in helping people? The help people receive from people—in this case professionally trained people who work on egocentric assumptions—is very limited. Whatever benefits accrue are shallow and temporary, because the basic problem, the god-problem, is not addressed. Whatever temporary benefits occur can be explained by the use of human willpower which, like the battery in a car, will move the car a short distance but then stop.

b. *God can no longer be deliberately excluded from the counseling process.*

We have already spoken of our unconscious exclusion of God which takes place quietly and effectively by the assumption of human omni-competence. I must add now that not all of it is unconscious. Some of it is deliberate and calculated.

It is no secret that most professional counselors look

upon a reference to God as a throwback to primitive infantilism. God is often rejected, sometimes attacked, and at other times ignored in such counseling. A man once came before the discharge staff of a hospital and was asked what benefit he had received from treatment. After a moment of reflection, he quietly reported that he had found God at this hospital and now he felt much better. A psychiatrist responded, "What is all this nonsense about God? God can only take you so far, then psychiatry must take over."

The patient afterward said that he felt like punching that doctor in the nose. I must confess to a similar reaction, until I realized that twelve years ago I believed the very same thing. Indeed, most clergymen, as well as psychiatrists, today believe that the God-approach to emotional illness will help a little, but when the going really gets tough, psychiatry must be called in.

The proof for this assertion is that whenever a parishioner begins to have real problems, the clergyman quickly refers the person into the hands of a "good psychiatrist" who, with his skill and training, begins to really help this person who is breaking down. The pastor now retreats to his comfortable study and offers a prayer of thanksgiving that God has again seen fit to use these "human means" to save his people.

On such a basis, one can easily understand the passion with which so many clergymen seek out the blessing and guidance of psychiatrists and psychologists. The clergyman keenly desires contact with them, asks to be taught by them, and hopefully aspires to possibly do a little bit of what they do. Why? Because *real* help for people is thought to come from man, autonomous man, man who has no place for God as the authority and power in his life.

There are numerous illustrations of ways in which we have excluded God from counseling. I have already spoken of our conscious doubt that God can do much for a severe case of emotional illness. I would like, however, to mention two other ways in which modern, humanistic psychotherapy counters God.

Except for a minority group of Christian and Jewish psychotherapists, the modern practitioners of mental science refuse to acknowledge the existence of any moral code external to a person. Values and ethics are one's own private business, and one is encouraged to hammer out what he thinks is right and good for himself, regardless of what external authorities—and God is one of them—have said. To be sure, one must be careful about getting thrown into jail, but if you can get away with it, do it. One person with such an individualistic ethic said to me, "Nobody—but nobody—is going to tell me what is right for me. I'll decide that." Exit God. Enter Self.

Another way in which I must part company with my colleagues in humanistic psychotherapy is in their incessant impugning of human authority. Modernly, for example, the major problems of the individual are assigned to the faulty training of his closest human authorities: his parents. I have before me an article which typically faults the parents for not really listening to their children, for not treating them with respect. "If he yells, you didn't listen when he talked." The punch line goes, "If the parent will give up the defensive and accept blame when the child has problems, a major obstacle to good relationship will have been overcome." The article concludes with a hope that someday, when the child grows up and points out the faults of his parents, the parents will be honest enough to admit their sins.

One is reminded of certain TV dramas which depict family life. I cannot claim wide knowledge of these programs, but it appears to me that the father in these dramas is always being taught the deep lessons of life by his children. I have seen several scenes in which the father is in the center of the living room, defending himself against the accusations of his all-wise son.

Finally the father breaks down, admits his errors, and is forgiven by that self-righteous little son.

Such an attitude, whether on TV or in the office of a psychotherapist, seems to me to do harm to people. It places them in opposition to human authority which God Himself established to represent Him. This is not a question, first of all, of dishonoring God or of being disrespectful to authority. I am sure God could not care less whether He is being treated respectfully. What He is concerned about is the damage which opposition to authority does to the person giving such opposition. We are damaged, not God. That is why God is so against disobedience to authority. That is why we should quickly come under the authority of God and human advisers. It is only when human authority is in conflict with God's authority that we must disobey it. Otherwise, to obey human authority is to obey God—and add this: it is an act which benefits us primarily.

For this reason, we should be encouraged to respect and honor all authority. In the counseling room, the counselor should stand with authority and encourage the counselee to come to terms with authorities. It may be necessary to forgive them, and it will certainly be necessary to express gratitude to them, but judgment and condemnation are simply the manifestation of an unresolved god-problem.

I am aware that the psychological authorities encourage us to express our anger, resentments, and condemnation against our authorities. It is felt that these feelings, when they are blocked, damage one's emotional health. Therefore, express your feelings, they say. Thousands of people are presently gathered into sensivity and encounter groups to help them get these feelings out, particularly the negative ones, for they do us damage, we are told.

In this way, people are trained to become more angry and more condemnatory. There is only superficial benefit from these exercises in emotional ventilation. There is another way to deal with the feelings,

I believe, a better way. It is the way of confession and with it, surrender.

c. *Counseling, if it is to have any deep and lasting effect, must include the suggestion to confess our sins and the suggestion to surrender the self to God.*

Yesterday I sat down with Doris. Here is the way our conversation went:

Doris: I'm terribly upset. Last night one of the patients attempted suicide, and there was such a commotion on the wards, I could not sleep all night. Please— let's not talk about this. Talking about suicide upsets me terribly.

Earl: We will talk about only what you are ready to bring up. Perhaps there is something else on your mind that is of greater concern to you.

Doris: I don't know what's wrong with me. Nothing seems to be working out right. Here I am, a college graduate, doing something I really like—teaching children—but still I feel like a failure. I'm a teacher— so what? And now this breakdown. When they brought me to the hospital, I did not even know who I was. I was out. I can't remember when I was so bad, except maybe when I had my abortion. Oh God, I still feel guilty about that. I can't stop thinking about it.

Earl: Would you like God's forgiveness for the abortion?

Doris: (quickly) Oh, yes! It's like a heavy weight around my neck.

Earl: Listen closely then to what I am going to say. You have already confessed your sin to God in my presence, and now I tell you, as one who is representing God, that your sin is forgiven.

Doris: But that's so easy!

Earl: You want to make it difficult?

Doris: No—not really.

Earl: I want to say it again. You have confessed your sin, and God has forgiven you. The matter is closed.

You need never accuse yourself or feel guilty of this again.

Doris: I guess I feel that I have to do something on my part—maybe something to show that I'm really sincere.

Earl: God knows you are sincere, Doris. But there is one thing you can do.

Doris: Oh, I *want* to.

Earl: I wonder if you are at a point where you are ready to ask God to come in and take control of your life. So far, Doris has tried very hard to control Doris. But you are not doing so well. Things keep going out of control—sexually, emotionally, and financially. (She had told me she was heavily in debt.) When a person tries to be in control, he goes out of control until he comes under control—God.

Are you ready for God as the Control of your life?

Doris: Gee, I frankly don't know. I . . . I don't know what to say.

Earl: Please don't say anything right now. Think it over a few days. I'll be around here and when you have reached some conclusions, let me know. We are going to be close friends, no matter what or when you decide.

My strategy was based on an assumption that the basic problem of life is moral and spiritual. Moral—because sin is involved. Spiritual—because the living God is involved. I have found this to be a simple and highly effective approach.

Confession and surrender are effective approaches because they depend completely on God. Take God out, and these methods collapse immediately.

I want a method so dependent upon God that it will fail completely without Him. And when the method succeeds, I want it to be only because of Him.

And this method is so simple! The popular professional approaches used to treat emotionally ill people are not simple. These approaches grow increasingly more complicated and difficult to understand.

Now, we would all be willing to overlook the basic deficiences in the world of behavioral science if only their strategies worked for suffering people. By any objective standard, however, the benefits are marginal at best.

Maybe—just maybe—the whole world may be ready for something as simple as God.

d. *The day of the professional counselor may soon be finished.*

I am a professional counselor. I am trained both in theology and psychology, and I am paid for what I do. As a professional, I need not ask "for whom the bell tolls." It tolls for me. I do not regret my professional death, because, like E. Stanley Jones, "I am alive in the Alive!" Beyond theology and psychology is God.

Frankly, I am relieved and now experience peace. The alliance between religion and psychology is unified in their insistence that we can somehow work our way into emotional health—and if we can't do it alone, we can pay to have someone help us work. We are encouraged to work through our feelings, work on a positive self-image, work on correct thinking, work out a philosophy of life that fits me, work on what seems right for me—work, work, work. Work hard also to pay the therapist who has worked himself almost to death for the proper diplomas and certificates. This professional will now combine his efforts with the suffering person to make the assault on Mount Never-rest. Work, climb, push—I'm relieved to sit down and rest in God.

This work-frenzy is predicated on a deep feeling that we must do something about ourselves. We ask: What must I *do* to be happy? These may be our questions, but they are surely not the questions of Jesus Christ. He is not interested in having us do any more. We've done it! The situation is bad enough! Christ does not want us to do anything except believe in Him.

What does it mean to believe in Christ? It means

that we no longer believe in ourselves, particularly in that presumptuous nonsense that we can save ourselves by hard work. Believing in Christ means to give up on ourselves as saviors of ourselves and turn to a true Savior. Belief in Christ entails really only one thing from us—obedience.

Obedience is the last thing that any of us gives Jesus Christ. We will give Him anything but that. We will work our fingers to the bone, lose ourselves in service to others, strive for moral perfection and knock ourselves out with Bible-reading, praying, and church-going, but obedience? Anything but that!

I was talking once to one of my parishioners who had recently surrendered his life to Christ. His name was Harold, and we were speaking about the need to become obedient to Christ as Lord.

"Yeah," said Harold, "makes me think of my aged mother. Maybe twenty years ago she said to me, 'Harold, there are thousands of words in the dictionary, and you know most all of them, but there is one little word that you never learned. I so hoped you would learn it, but you never did. That one little word is *obey*.'"

"It's the toughest word, I'm sure," I responded, "but you are beginning to learn it."

"Somewhat," said Harold, "but I have a long way to go."

"Would you like to learn more about obedience?"

Harold reflected. "Yes, I want to be obedient to Christ, but I don't know how to begin."

"Then let me help you. Tell me, is your mother still alive?"

"Yes. She is in her eighties."

"I have a suggestion, Harold. Why don't you call her tonight and tell her that you have finally discovered the meaning of the word *obey*. She'll remember. Let her know that her son has learned the basic lesson of life before she goes to her grave."

"I will. She deserves to know that."

Well, Harold was obedient to Christ through my suggestion. When the dear old lady heard about Harold's obedience, she broke down and wept tears of joy and thanksgiving.

No question about it—Harold knows the meaning of that little word *obey*.

Let me return to the matter of work and the professional. I have a dear friend who happens to be a Christian and a psychiatrist. He takes a position which is fairly representative of most Christian psychiatrists. His reasoning goes like this: "Most emotional cripples are so hung up that the claims of the Gospel of Jesus Christ cannot even penetrate to them. These sick people have all kinds of defensive barriers which must be broken down if ever Christ is to get through to them. Once they are freed from their neurotic defenses and inhibiting complexes, they are in shape to hear about God. Psychotherapy makes it possible for one to be open to God."

At this point, I asked my brother if he then proceeded to invite his patients to surrender their lives to God. "Oh no," he responded, "it is not ethical for me to go that far. I don't see it as my task to explain the message of Jesus Christ to him. What I do is refer the patient to his pastor."

I have difficulties with this position. First, when a sick person reaches out in good faith to a psychiatrist, that person assumes that he will be given help—not that he is being prepared to receive help. I have questions about feeding the hopes of the patient that he will receive help and then when he is ready to receive it, the basic help is withheld from him until a referral can be made to another helper. At the least, the patient should be informed of this arrangement before treatment begins.

And why should *not* a Christian psychiatrist lead his patient to God? Anyone who knows God and withholds the knowledge of Him from a suffering person is guilty of depriving a hungry person of a great feast, preferring rather to feed him the crumbs of human resource. Dr. Paul Tournier, the famous Swiss psychiatrist, surely does not hold back with his patients. He tells them about God, hears confessions, invites his patients to surrender to God, also prays with them. So I said to my friend, "Be a Paul Tournier."

Finally, as a counseling pastor, I find I really do not need (and I suspect, neither does God need it) all this psychiatric preparation for the encounter with God. One comes to God just as one is. We come to Him loaded with anxiety, inner protest, suffering from a multitude of unknown bondages, and usually staggering under a weight of fatigue which is so heavy that it hurts. God wants us that way. He uses our pain to bring us to Him. Take the pain away, and we probably won't come. Most psychiatrists are sworn enemies of pain—a fact proven by their immediate and constant use of sedatives and tranquilizers.

My point is as simple as this—suffering people are basically in need of God, not of the professionals. Our godlessness is exposed by the idolatrous faith we have placed in professional counselors, both psychiatric and pastoral.

A long, long time ago, a man called Moses made an announcement to the members of his nation. Moses said, "Jehovah has said that henceforth we are to worship Him without the use of handmade idol images. From now on, nothing in between—just you and God."

I can almost hear the reaction of the children of Israel: "This new law will never work! Any fool knows you need an idol-image to make contact with Jehovah. We need both—the idol-image and Jehovah. One needs the other, and we need both. Moses! We warn you, a lot of innocent people are going to be led astray if you do away with these beautiful images. God uses such means!"

Religion and psychiatry are our modern idols. Few people entertain any doubts that these idols will save us. "What would we do without them?" they ask. The answer to that question is that all we would have left would be a living God. This is all God wants us to have —Him. "Thou shalt have no other gods before me."

I sense the beginning of a turning from the idolatry of professionals in the impressive rise of lay groups which really minister to the needs of people. Increasingly, we are being ministered to by laymen whose healed lives bear testimony to the validity of their way. The credentials of wide learning and academic accomplishments still satisfy most people in our culture, but some of us are beginning to see that the days of the professional helper may be numbered. Currently, it is heresy to say that. For this opinion, some of us risk being cast out of the temples dedicated to the glory of man. We are accused of running away from the accepted truth. It is an open question, however, who is running—the whole world or God's people? Remember that "in a world of fugitives, the person heading in the opposite direction appears to be running away" (e.e. cummings).

If it is true that man is in flight from God, then it is time to turn back to God, even though this appears foolish to our fellow travelers.

8

God's Way of Entering His Kingdom

Truly, truly, I say to you, unless one is born anew, he cannot see the kingdom of God. (John 3:3)

A few days ago, I saw a young boy crying as he waited in a car at the entrance of the hospital where I work. I asked him what was wrong.

Sobbing, he said, "My father is bringing my mother here for a few weeks. She drinks too much."

I can't tell you what sympathy I felt for this crying boy. He dearly loved his mother, but she was an alcoholic.

I identify closely with that boy, because my Mother, the pseudo-religious church of Christ, is a spiritual alcoholic. The children of Mother Church are shattered by what has happened to her. We love this Mother, deeply and tenderly. But our Mother is drunk. It hurts terribly to say that. We hate to hear our own words. There was a time, perhaps, when we lashed out at her in judgment and anger, but no longer. It is too late for that. Our love forbids it. All we can now feel is pity and pain.

The children of Mother Church, however, are doubly

desolate. Our human father, psychological science, while promising to help us with our deepest life-problems, has also failed us. Our human father has defaulted in his responsibility to lead us to God, the source of true help. At other times, this father has given us advice and counsel which sent us down roads which led nowhere. Worst of all, our psychiatrist father has harmed us by such things as encouraging us in egocentric living, the avoidance of problems through medication, and a pseudo-neutrality regarding moral conduct.

Our human parents have forsaken us. A long time ago a man said, "For my father and my mother have forsaken me, but the Lord will take me up" (Ps. 27:10), yet we ask—how? *How* are we to find a way into the Kingdom of God if not through these venerable parents? Who will instruct us if not they? Who will teach us the deep secrets of life if not the theologians and the behavioral scientists?

Well, first of all, be assured that God has not abandoned His children. There is a way into the Kingdom of God—into that Kingdom where God will bring us into an undreamed of liberation from our bondages and additionally, give us the blessings of peace of mind and joy of spirit.

Who will teach us the way to enter into and live in the Kingdom of God?

God's way of entering the Kingdom of God is being taught us today, it seems to me, by the Kingdom-people whose shattered lives are being renewed by the power of God. If we may for a moment speak of these people as the "winners," then we may say, "Seek out the winners and receive instruction from these amazing people as to how to enter the Kingdom of God."

Seek the instruction of the *winners*—not the glib talkers whose smooth words are offered only to impress us.

Seek the instruction of the *winners*—not the sophisticated intellectual whose eight-cylinder brain still has not found a way to get his stalled life into gear.

Seek the instruction of the *winners*—not those busy-bodies whose activism leaves nothing for God to do except stand on the sidelines of their lives and applaud at appropriate intervals.

Seek the instruction of the *winners*—not that company of experts who are so quick to hand you their untested solutions, knowing full well they will never need to live with the results.

Seek the instruction of the *winners*—not the play-actors who look so pious and so sincere in hopes that this will permit them to test their ideas in your life.

Who, then, are these winners?

They are people whose lives were broken, wasted, shattered—but people whose lives, by the power of God, are now mending, healing, and growing.

That cannot be faked. Knowledge can be faked. Feelings can be faked. Intentions can be faked. But a resurrection from the dead cannot be faked. Either one is alive and growing in freedom, peace, and joy, or one is dead, entombed in various bondages and existing (but not living) in a pervasive mood of sadness, depression, and conflict.

Right now I'm thinking of two winners from among several hundred that I could choose.

Let me briefly describe Nanette first. She is a twenty-four-year-old woman who was drug addicted, spent time in jail on several occasions, and then took up residence in a mental hospital because of her emotional problems. When I saw her on the hospital ward, she was chaos personified. What particularly struck me was the hard, tough look on her face. Her one redeeming feature was a good figure, but her face was not attractive. Home life consisted of a continual war with her father. Nanette was a loser any way you looked at her.

Upon discharge from the hospital, Nanette was referred into the hands of Christine who had had a marvelous experience of spiritual renewal. And that's when it all happened. Christine excitedly told Nanette what had happened to her. The spiritual needs of Nanette were so great that she surrendered to Christ. Within a few weeks, we began to see the beginning of a dramatic life-change. Nanette came into the Kingdom of God.

It is now a year and a half since Nanette's discharge. She is a renewed person. How do we know? Well, first of all, look at her face: She's beautiful now. She could hardly fake that. She is also off of drugs. How do we know? Because she associates with other recovering drug addicts, and if she was using drugs, they would spot it immediately. Finally, her father speaks with utter amazement about the new Nanette and their close relationship. These realities could hardly be faked by Nanette.

Nanette is a winner. She has answers which are validated in her life. She is the kind of person from whom we can safely receive good instruction about life. "I can sum it all up," she says, "in one word—God."

Max is another person I can present as a winner. He *was* a walking disaster—drugs, alcohol, sexual perversion, marital discord, trouble with the law. One day, a broken, tired Max gave up and surrendered his life to God. Today, he is winning over these problems. They are arrested. A week ago, a severely crippled neurotic told me how Max had been the means unto his recovery. This, again, could not be faked. Max is a winner. His new way of life proves that he knows the way into the Kingdom of God. Max is *there.*

If you need more examples, go to the thousands who have found God through the testimony of the Billy Graham Crusades, Campus Crusades for Christ, many evangelical churches, the Jesus People, Alcoholics Anonymous, and most recently, the growing company of charismatic Christians. People whose changed lives prove that they are in the Kingdom of God are the people who deserve commendation to us as safe guides into the Kingdom. Distrust all others.

I have tried to be a student of these winners since my own entrance into the Kingdom of God about twelve years ago. What constantly impresses me is the similarity and unity of the case histories. True, each person's problems are different as to detail, but not as to the fundamental nature of the problem. This is because the problem is one problem, not many. All problems seem to be reducible to one problem, and its nature is basically spiritual. It follows that if there is only one fundamental problem, then we need look for only one solution. In this, we follow the ancient wisdom of the Bible which defines one human problem (sin) and announces one solution to that problem (God in Christ).

The point I wish to make now, however, is that we can discern certain definite stages which the winners go through as they go from the problem to its solution. Consider the following stages in the journey from the Kingdom of Self into the Kingdom of God:

Stage 1—The Long Period of Unendurable Pain. The egocentric world we construct becomes increasingly hellish. We go out of control. Our world also goes out of control. The pain produced by this kind of suffering is so unproductive. It accomplishes nothing but fatigue.

Stage 2—The Losing Struggle Against Inner Bondage. This struggle goes on concurrently with the long Period of Unendurable Pain. A continuing attempt is made to gain mastery over ourselves and our world. It is assumed that man has the power, if only he decides to be strong and use his I-will-power. Increasingly, it becomes apparent that the battle is being lost. We continue to lose ground.

Stage 3—Naming and Accepting the Bondage. The lives of the winners reveal that this is the earliest step in the direction of a change. No one moves toward change until he names, admits, and then accepts his bondage(s). This stage is usually reached only because the evidence of bondage is so overwhelming and damning that a denial of the evidence can be maintained only at the risk of being called insane. Not wishing to have such a label tacked on us, we choose the lesser evil of accepting a problem. The lives of the winners show that it usually takes years before a person comes to this Level.

Stage 4—The Agonizing Choice. One can both admit and accept his bondage but nonetheless choose to continue in it. Many people dearly love their bondage. Try curing all the imagined illnesses of a hypochrondriac and see what an unhappy person you have on your hands.

If one has, however, reached the sickening point and sincerely wishes to be free, an agonizing choice now opens up to the person. Either he can choose the Kingdom of Self and remain in bondage, or he can come into the Kingdom of God and be set free.

Stage 5—The Act of Surrendering One's Will to God. Kingdom-people may not always have a clear recollection of that point in their lives when finally they ended their war with God, but *that* they surrendered is clearly understood by them. As Dag Hammarskjold said:

I don't know Who—or what—put the question, I don't know when it was put. I don't even remember answering. But at some moment I did answer YES to Someone—or Something—and from that hour I was certain that existence is meaningful and that, therefore, my life, in self-surrender, had a goal.*

The initial act of surrender must be followed by a continuing surrender of one's will and one's life. Our surrender is done by degrees. It is a tedious process. Certain areas of our lives we will give up, but not

*Dag Hammarskjold, *Markings* (New York: Knopf, 1965) p. 205.

others. King Self will at times surrender something and then immediately reclaim it. Christ our King is infinitely patient with us as we procrastinate and yield, cooperate and rebel, relinquish and take back. All the old tricks which King Self learned in his earliest years are dragged out for yet another boring recital. How dull—and fruitless!

Stage 6—The Act of Confession. Suddenly, upon surrender, the conscience becomes quickened. The presence of God in one's life makes this unavoidable. It is a mark of good training and real character to feel guilt not only over wrongdoing, but particularly for the way in which we denied a place for God in our lives. Confession is simply becoming reconciled to God by means of real honesty and a dependency upon God's mercy. It seems that the winners in the Kingdom of God all have this healing act in their case histories in one form or another.

Stage 7—The Act of Prayer. It is interesting but sad that people outside the Kingdom of God often have great difficulty speaking to God. Small wonder!—He is the hated enemy. We usually give God the silent treatment until we make peace with Him. Finally our sealed lips begin to speak a few words—perhaps a request—perhaps a word of gratitude—to the One who, we now realize, has always loved us. That is prayer. Prayer becomes increasingly spontaneous on the lips of winners.

Stage 8—The Act of Taking Things Back. Sometimes this means restoring stolen goods to the rightful owner. It may also mean taking back cruel words we have spoken about another. This would be done through an apology. My files are filled with instances where new citizens of the Kingdom of God have taken things back.

One man, as a youth, stole a gear from a tanning factory. Twenty years later, he wished to apologize and make restitution. The factory had moved to a new location, but he tracked them down and sent them a note of apology with twenty-five dollars. The tanning company was so surprised to find this kind of honesty still alive that they sent him one of their nicest sheepskins.

Stage 9—The Act of Continually Caring for Oneself. This is where so many of God's people fall flat on their faces. We often fail to really keep our lives under control because we feel no need for a continual program of nurture in the spiritual way of life. Yet we know that no matter how dramatic one's entrance into the Kingdom of God, if a person fails to keep his life under Authority as it is mediated to him by other people under Authority, the return to bondage will not be long in coming. Surrender to God is not a once-for-all-time event. It must be repeatedly acted out with a spiritual adviser.

Stage 10—The Act of Thanking God for the Bondages. This goes beyond even that climactic act of Pierre D'Harcourt when he kissed his chains while a prisoner. That act indicated acceptance and brought him deep peace. Thanking God for our bondage assumes an acceptance of our bondages but then goes on to realize that they have become a great blessing to us. What we thought was a bitter lemon has been turned into lemonade! I hear the winners say—"I thank God I am a recovering neurotic." "I had to become an alcoholic to learn the lessons I needed to learn." "Thank God I went to jail—where else would I take time to think?"

Stage 11—The Act of Reaching Out to Others. At this point, the winner reaches out to others who need his help. He waits to help, lends assistance when it is requested, and probably most importantly, shares his life-story with the person in need. Such testimonies have a truthful ring to them. They are authentic. These witnesses carry a kind of authority with which it is difficult to argue.

Such reaching out to others will always be free from the charge of do-goodism because this action is basically done to help oneself. This is not egoism. It is the

140

essence of kingdom living when two people care equally for each other under God.

You noticed, I am sure, that at every stage except the first and second, the winners go into action. This is a crucial point. We *act* out of our problems. It is folly to think our way out. No one ever comes into the Kingdom of God who is bogged down in a think-trap, asking the impossible-to-answer questions Why? and How? The way out of the think-trap—and let us add, the feeling-trap—is to go into action.

About a dozen years ago, when the bottom was dropping out of my life, it got through to me that if I was to be saved from the torture of my own think-traps and feeling-traps, I must act. Act, that is, obediently to God. But how?

My recovering alcoholic parishioners offered an answer to that question: "What we do is get ourselves a sponsor; we begin to make the meetings; we work the program. That's how we go into action."

Fine. Fine for alcoholics, but I didn't have the right qualifications for membership in AA.

I guess God knew the guidance I needed, because a plan began to form in my mind. Perhaps I could ask a close friend to be my spiritual adviser. I might be helped if I sat down regularly with him and worked along the lines of the twelve steps of AA. And why would it not work to ask this brother for advice and counsel both as to what I had done, what I am now doing, and what I plan to do? The idea grew, thanks to the Holy Spirit and my quiet desperation.

I've already described the basic need in all of us for a relationship with a spiritual adviser. I have a few more thoughts to add because a spiritual adviser is nothing less than a key directly into the Kingdom of God.

The first few rides with my spiritual guide were quite bumpy. He felt my ideas were much too Roman Catholic, particularly this business of speaking a confession to God in his presence. I must admit that the first time I did this, I felt my Protestant gears grinding. But now I have come to have a deep conviction that we Protestants made a tragic and costly mistake four hundred years ago when we stopped using the confessional. The winners I know use it.

Why is it so important that I have a spiritual adviser listen as I confess my sins to God? There are many good reasons* but I will mention only one. Once one really discloses his life to God, there is need to receive counsel as to how to go into action on taking things back (which we already discussed under Stage 8). I cannot overstate the damage one does if he advises himself after confession. Such a person will either be overly punitive, or make needless efforts at self-atonement, or possibly autosuggest absurd attempts at apology or restitution. The one who advises himself cannot escape unconsciously using his egocentric perspective which, though it is disguised as the epitome of reason and good logic, is full of folly.

The reason we abhor the counsel of a spiritual adviser is clear and understandable: we do not want anyone crossing our wills. We do not want anyone getting in our way and messing up our plans. Confirmation and support we always accept, but not anything which counters our wills. Not only will we decide what to do, but the idea must originate with us.

So no matter how pious the penitent, if he insists on still going his own way, he is still playing god and has evicted God from his world. It's that simple. If I advise myself, I am no longer under the will of God. I am under my own will, no matter how many times I mumble, "Thy will be done on earth as it is in heaven."

After I have tried to be open and honest to God in the presence of my spiritual adviser, the first thing he does is speak on behalf of Christ. In Christ's name, he forgives my sins. Is not that what we are supposed to do? "If you forgive the sins of any, they are forgiven"

*The author has discussed the benefits of auricular confession more fully in his book *The God Players* (Grand Rapids, Mich.: Zondervan, 1970), pp. 111-114.

(John 20:23), said Jesus. And how can anyone speak that word of forgiveness to me unless he hears what I have confessed? I can't tell you how much I need to hear my brother say to me, "Earl, Christ forgives you. Now let go of it. It's finished business. Let it rest. Be assured of God's pardon."

It is right at this point that I stand in need of counsel. My guilt has been pardoned, but there may still need to be some further steps to take in the direction of restoring what I have wrongfully taken or apologizing for what I have said, or becoming reconciled to people with whom I am at odds—to mention just a few of the things which need to be done. I am the world's poorest judge of what I now ought to do, because I am the blindest person in the world when it comes to my own egoism. Let me give an example.

I once confessed to a resentment toward a certain person to whom I am distantly related. I had always kept plenty of distance between us for a number of what I now realize were foolish, petty reasons. My opinion of this person had always been rather low, and this I now felt was an unjustified judgment. I told my spiritual adviser that I intended to write a letter of apology to this person.

My adviser questioned me closely on several points and then asked if he might make a suggestion. I asked for it. He gave it to me—and it went like this: "I disagree with you about sending a letter. You told me that this other person feels no need for an apology as far as you know. (This was true.) Secondly, what this person needs is a visit at your first opportunity, not a piece of paper. Also, you sound a little over-scrupulous to me, so check yourself for your old problem of moral perfectionism. Finally, I suggest we both think this matter over a bit more and look at it again at our next visit. Meanwhile, I suggest you do nothing."

My will, you see, had been countered. My counselor made no decisions for me—he only differed, giving me the freedom to choose any course. Either way, he would still accept and love me.

After eight years of living under this kind of spiritual discipline, I have learned to follow the suggestions of my adviser unless what he suggests is absolutely immoral or obviously indecent—which it never is. Most times I happen to agree with his advice, but even in those cases where I disagree with it, I usually still act on his suggestions because: (1) my perception of reality is screened by my egoism; (2) he has my best interests at heart; (3) this arrangement provides a concrete way for me to actualize the will of God in my life; and (4) I like very much the results I see in my life as a result of the path of obedience.

Of course, all of this takes time. My spiritual guide and I get together on a regular basis—never longer than three-week intervals between appointments. We use the phone and meet by special arrangement in between regular appointments. Future appointments must always be set by the time I leave my adviser, else I find that my egoism prevails, and months go by in which I am flying solo—straight for the side of a mountain.

One day, not too long after I had begun the practice of confession, I asked my spiritual adviser who he went to for confession and spiritual advice. "I confess my sins to God but have no one from whom I seek advice." This was honest, if not commendable. I sensed immediately that from this theological view of the world, things ended with him. Others like myself might need spiritual discipline, but he was above that. He was, I imagined, some kind of a pope to whom others would come for help, but there was no one to whom he would go for help.

Well, we talked about this matter. He seemed surprised when I told him that the current pope in Rome goes to confession every week, using a bishop as his spiritual adviser. Finally, in this devious way, I got to my question: Was he ready for a spiritual adviser in his life? I asked this out of concern for him but also for myself. There were real doubts in my mind about anything other than an intellectual submission to Christ on his part if there was no concrete human person through whom to become obedient. I was concerned for myself as well. If he were to continue to respond to my request for counsel out of the "wisdom" of his own egocentric life, I knew we could not continue, for he would return me to the bondage of Earl.

My good brother thought over my question and said he was ready. With that, I suggested we experiment with being spiritual advisers to each other, each using forty-five minutes at our regular meetings. The experiment is now finished. We are convinced that this is a marvelously effective way for human beings to live and care for themselves. We are a micro-church experiencing the macro-life of God as we are safely guided from one exciting day to the next.

Even though Mother Church and Father Behavioral Science have forsaken us, it is still possible for any of us children to enter into the Kingdom of God. The winners show us the Way. I have tried their Way, once I had abandoned all other ways, and found that this Way could straighten out my life. I have seen God do this same miracle in the lives of hundreds of troubled, anxious, despairing people who had reached The End and were finally ready for God. He wants us all to enter the Kingdom of God. God has given us the keys to His Kingdom. I would like to make a few simple suggestions as to concrete steps anyone can take to enter into this Kingdom which is eternal.

1. *Name your bondage.* Complete this sentence: "I am a _____ ." By such a statement, we confess our sin. For more detailed instructions, consult Chapter 4, part 2—"The Bondage of the Self to Self."

2. *Surrender your will and your life to God.* I urge you, if you have not yet asked God to be your King, to

take this decisive step right now. Place your life under a New Manager with this prayer:

Father in Heaven:

I will resist you no longer. I give up. You take over my life and run it according to Your will.

By Your divine power, straighten out my life and lead me into freedom.

I submit myself to Your divine authority. If at any time in the future I fall into sin, or begin to doubt, or even deny You—disregard my rebellion.

Let the covenant we are making now stand eternally.

In the Name of Jesus Christ, my Lord. Amen.

3. *Ask the Holy Spirit to guide you to a spiritual adviser.* Not just anyone, as you can well imagine, will do as a spiritual adviser. I think I speak the mind of the Holy Spirit in pointing out four things to avoid in selecting this person:

a. Avoid a brand-new convert, because he lacks foundation in the faith.

b. Avoid having many spiritual advisers, because we will use one against the other.

c. Avoid using a spouse as a spiritual adviser, because it is confusing for a marriage partner to play a number of different roles with us. There are times, to be sure, when we will turn to a spouse for spiritual advice, but normally this role is better carried by another Christian.

d. Avoid having a spiritual adviser from the opposite sex, because you have enough troubles without asking for more.

I refer you, however, to the leading of the Holy Spirit in this matter. When we ask Him to guide us to a spiritual adviser, He will not mislead us, for it is a good thing which we ask.

4. *When you have been guided to a particular person, I suggest you begin along these lines:*

a. Ask him to read this chapter and ascertain whether he is in general agreement with its contents.

b. Tell him that you have taken steps 1, 2, and 3 above. Spell out each one. This is very important. In this public disclosure of your relationship to God, you are sealing an understanding at which you and God have arrived privately. All this has the greatest present and eternal significance.

c. Invite your friend to form a triangle, each being a spiritual adviser to the other. God is at the apex of the triangle. By this simple arrangement, you give up your egocentric status.

5. *Begin spoken confession to God with your spiritual adviser regarding past actions, present involvements, and future plans.* Agree to have a confidential relationship. This gives you complete freedom to speak the truth. Having been honest with God and your adviser, you are now ready to receive counsel from God through your mentor.

6. *Pray together.* It is time we begin talking to the One we have opposed so long. Time also to call Him by His unique Name—Lord Jesus Christ. It is past time to give thanks for all He has done for us. It is time to let our requests be known to Him. It is time.

7. *Come to agreements between yourselves in God's presence.* Accept the advice and counsel of your spiritual adviser. Come to agreements between yourselves, for these contracts are the keys into the Kingdom of God. God has given us these keys. They are binding agreements arrived at between you and your spiritual adviser in the presence of God.

8. *Be open to the guidance of God in your life through the following means:*

a. "Our general guidance is the life and character and teaching of Jesus Christ . . . "

b. "God guides through the counsel of good people."

c. "God guides through an opening providence."

d. "God guides through your heightened moral intelligence."

e. "God guides through the inner voice."*

*The foregoing "means" are taken from E. Stanley Jones, *Song of Ascents* (New York: Abingdon 1968), p. 188-189.

It is important that you do not try to figure out the will of God. It is God's problem to get through to you, so stop trying to do His work. He uses the above means —usually in the order given. Egocentrics use the last means first.

9. *Meet with your spiritual adviser by appointment on a regular basis.* Only by this means can we avoid the greatest pitfall of those who finally find God. It is possible to find God and then lose Him. We lose Him when, failing to invite a discipline to function over us, we revert back to playing god. God is immediately dead to us when we choose the path of disobedience to His will.

10. *Give thought to enlarging your fellowship to include other needy people.* As you invited one into fellowship with you, now both of you invite still another person. Share your experience with the newcomer and offer to be an adviser to him. Do not look for people who might enjoy this sort of thing. Never mind the comfortable people who say they have no problems. Rather, go to God's suffering people. "Those that are well have no need of a physician, but those who are sick; I came not to call the righteous, but sinners" (Mark 2:17). So call the sick sinners into your fellowship.

It is my belief that God is making known to us twentieth-century Christians a new (and yet, very first-century-ish) way of entering into and then being nurtured in the Kingdom of God. I am convinced that Alcoholics Anonymous is one group—although by no means the only group—who will have much to teach us about this way. There are now a half million of these people throughout the world who (1) have worked a spiritual program—the twelve steps—which leads them straight to God; (2) have found freedom from one of the very worst forms of human bondage; (3) have experienced a serenity and joy in living which is a proof of the presence of God in their lives; (4) are effectively reaching out to a large group of very needy people who have problems similar to their own; and (5) continue to grow in a way of life which is basically God-centered.

Why could not you and I, with our numerous non-alcoholic kinds of alcoholisms, also have such a program, such a fellowship, and such results in our lives? Where is that simple, effective organization which could be God's saving instrument for that great multitude of people who right now are crying out for a true freedom from their bondage?

Let us, in these last moments together, hastily sketch a rough model of such a saving instrument.

I'm thinking of a fellowship of small groups. One would enter such a fellowship because of his suffering and need for renewal rather than because of intellectual assent to the guiding principles. The basic question would not be, Am I right? but rather, Do I want to get well and become a free person?

The only requirement for membership in such a gathering would be a desire to be free from one's personal bondages and to help others to the same freedom.

A major aim of this group would be to draw people by attraction rather than promotion.

Honesty with oneself, openness to others, and a basic reliance upon God as the source of power would characterize the group life. Members would witness to their experience of God's renewal of their lives rather than to a set of doctrinal teachings, valuable as they may be.

Such a fellowship would be well-advised to avoid owning property and handling money. These concerns always seem to have a way of diverting us from that single, simple purpose of coming into the Kingdom.

This group we are thinking about would not be allied with a particular denomination or sect but neither would it be in opposition to any. Indeed, this fellowship would function as a movement working cooperatively within many established bodies.

The group should be theocratic in its organization.

Elected leaders would be servants of the Lord to the group. The elected leadership would understand that in their offices, they are privileged to serve God's people rather than working for ego-satisfaction and the delights of using power upon people.

This group should be of one class, recognizing neither race, social status, professional standing, or previous reputation.

This fellowship would greatly profit from close contact with lay groups which already have a rich body of tradition and experience.

I believe God is at work today forming this kind of a fellowship for us. It is emerging. In the final chapter, of this book we'll see that the shape of this "new thing" is already discernible. God is no longer waiting. He is giving us what we need.

And it seems, we are finally *ready* for what we need.

9

The Power to Deliver

You shall receive power when the Holy Spirit has come upon you. (Acts 1:8)

Now that I have told you some of the disadvantages of living in the Kingdom of Self, let me also tell you about one great advantage.

The benefit of an egocentric life-style to King Self is that he becomes a lifelong devotee of power. It comes close to being an obsession with him. This obsession almost kills him, but God can also use it to lead the king to Himself.

King Self completely devoted himself throughout his life to acquiring power. From earliest childhood, he dreamed of controlling his world. Even supernatural power was called upon to support (but not control, thank you) the exciting destiny of himself as a god-king.

The results, we know all too well, were completely disastrous. It was because King Self was fascinated with *his own power.* He was right in that he needed power—but wrong in looking to himself as the source of that power.

This is the basic problem with all egocentrics: we lack the power to deliver ourselves from the power of evil. This is why we must turn away from the pseudo-religionists and the psychologists and turn to the God of all power.

This God—this God of all power—has a name.

He is the Holy Spirit.

Many egoists, when they are sick and tired of being sick and tired, ask for and receive the Holy Spirit and His power. That old obsessive fascination with power now leads the weary egoist straight to the source of all power in the Holy Spirit.

So thank God for our power-hungry egoism! But praise Him even more that the Holy Spirit is today dramatically filling our need for the power to be delivered from the Kingdom of Self. God is again revealing to us that the Holy Spirit is abundantly powerful to bring us into the Kingdom of His Son, Jesus Christ.

Just look around and see what is happening today. The Holy Spirit is falling upon God's people all over the world. A new Pentecost has come upon us as thousands upon thousands are receiving the Baptism in the Holy Spirit.

I rejoice to participate in the current charismatic revival.

Why?

Because I am a devotee of the divine person who possesses *all* power—the Holy Spirit.

I see the power of the Holy Spirit breathing the breath of life into mental patients who have surrendered to the Lord Jesus Christ.

I see the power of the Holy Spirit in that growing company of believers—Protestants, Roman Catholics, and Jews—so many of whom are obviously manifesting both the gifts and the fruits of the Holy Spirit.

I see the power of the Holy Spirit all over the world—

Indonesia, Korea, South America, Israel, Europe, even here in the Eastern United States where for so long we have lived in a spiritual desert.

A pastor friend of mine had for years been plowing the stony, spiritual soil of a number of churches in New York State. He came into contact with some turned-on charismatic Christians, receiving the Baptism in the Holy Spirit. Some time after this occurred, I received a phone call from him.

"Earl, can you give me an appointment? I need to see you as soon as possible." I receive many calls of this nature, so I pressed him a little to find out just how urgent his needs were.

"I need you to examine my head," he said without any hint of embarrassment. "My church board is sending me to you to find out whether I am psychotic. You see, some time ago I received the Baptism in the Holy Spirit—" and he went on to tell me how this had led to some grinding of the gears between the congregation and himself.

"Okay," I said, "you come down tomorrow, but there is something I must tell you. We'll have to find someone to examine my head, because I've also received the Holy Spirit."

So the pastor came. I examined his head—thoroughly and seriously—because pastors can become psychotic like anyone else. I think I know a diseased mind when I see one, but this fellow simply did not fit the picture. He was a solid person, emotionally stable, and wonderfully loving toward the church board who was sure he was crazy. No matter how I looked at this man, he was an impressive product of God's workmanship. After we had prayed together, we parted, praising the Lord for the power which had come into our lives.

It was the demonstrated power of the Holy Spirit in the lives of the Pentecostals and neo-Pentecostals which first drew me to them. I was extremely suspicious of these people in my first contacts with them. Like many other Christians, I had stubbed my toes on the phenomenon of speaking in tongues. It almost turned me back to my traditional understandings, tame and unexciting as they were. But praise the Holy Spirit, He eventually got through to me with this wild gift of speaking in tongues, once I had the humility and obedience to ask for it. It is not this gift, however, nor for that matter any of the other eight charisms of the Spirit mentioned in I Corinthians 12, which drew my interest. I was drawn to the Person behind the gifts. I am excited by the person of the Holy Spirit and His infinite power.

Only the Holy Spirit has the power to deliver us from our personal bondages. Only the Holy Spirit can lead us out of the Kingdom of Self into the Kingdom of God. Only the Holy Spirit can turn us away from pseudo-religion and humanistic psychology to become a new kind of people in the emerging church of today and tomorrow.

This is the day of charismatic renewal. I want to list a few characteristics which recommend this movement as an authentic work of the Holy Spirit in our day:

1. *The charismatic movement correctly understands that God is performing miracles today.* Most Christians, and I was among them, do not really believe that to be true.

We were told that the age of miracles ceased when the New Testament canon was completed. I was content to let it go at that until my investigation of God's miracles of healing through Oral Roberts, Kathryn Kuhlman, Alfred Price, and others showed the falsehood of that position. The Holy Spirit is obviously very eager to demonstrate His miraculous power among His people. I have come to understand that the only barrier to His miraculous work among us today is our unbelief—that is, we don't believe the Holy Spirit can and will work miracles today. As Matthew says, "He did not do many mighty works there, because of their unbelief" (Matt. 13:58).

How we need the Holy Spirit to perform His mighty

works in our mental hospitals. We do not need more hospital beds, more psychiatrists, nor staff, nor money, no, not even more chaplains. We need the Holy Spirit to resurrect the mentally ill from these medical centers called psychiatric hospitals.

2. *The movement of the Holy Spirit accurately discerns the spiritual nature of our basic problem in life.*

Most charismatics, following the teaching of that most unusual Chinese Christian, Watchman Nee, affirm the biblical teaching that man is composed of spirit, soul, and body. Modern psychology ignores man's spirit, because the behavioral scientists are so completely absorbed in the study of man's soul (intellect, will, and emotions). We are encouraged to develop our soulish powers by which to assert our mastery over life. Watchman Nee correctly discerned that this is the very worst mistake man can make. What we need is not soul-development but for our dead human spirits to be brought to life and joined by the Holy Spirit. We cannot really be helped until we are born of the Holy Spirit. Once our spiritual need is met by the Holy Spirit joining Himself to our spirits, a sure foundation for emotional health is laid.

What this means is that the problem with man is basically spiritual rather than psychological or genetic or environmental. We are human spirits who need the Holy Spirit. When "he who is united to the Lord becomes one spirit with him" (I Cor. 6:17), the basic life-problem is solved. How simple!

3. *Another thing that should commend the charismatic movement to us is the way Spirit-filled Christians are learning to submit themselves to temporal authority out of obedience to God.*

I had opportunity to study firsthand the charismatically oriented Community of Jesus in Orleans, Mass. The Holy Spirit has gathered a dozen households who have agreed to live in the Light in a fellowship of love and discipline. The Community is structured so that each member is subject to another member as a means of actualizing his obedience to Christ. New members are quickly assimilated, responding as they do to that most important fruit of the Holy Spirit: love. I was struck by the presence in the members of an authentic freedom (not to mention their joy and peace) in Christ which was given to them through submission to fellow Christians and ecclesiastical authority.

Other groups of charismatic Christians throughout the country are forming themselves under the discipline of the Holy Spirit. So far I have heard of the Hallelujah Community in Augusta, Georgia, the Church of the Redeemer in Houston, Texas, and the Word of God Community in Ann Arbor, Michigan. The latter is made up of about forty residential households, two-thirds of which are Roman Catholic families.

A Roman Catholic priest at the Seventh Annual International Conference on Charismatic Renewal reports how the Holy Spirit brought him into submission to God:

> The charismatic experience has completely changed my church politics and my national politics. I began to understand why it is that the Scriptures enjoin us to be submissive to those in authority over us. Now I'm totally in support of those in authority who minister order to the nations. Without that order, there'd be chaos and destruction.*

I rejoice that people as diverse as Roman Catholics (many of whom were beginning to defy ecclesiastical authority) and Baptists (many of whom rejected ecclesiastical authority) and brand-new converts (who had totally ignored ecclesiastical authority) are able to relate obediently and gladly to their various authorities for no other reason than that Jesus asked them to do this. There is a new voluntary submission among these people of the Holy Spirit, not only to ecclesiastical authority but to all legitimate temporal authority.

4. *One of the greatest contributions so far of the charismatic movement has been its serious recognition*

of the reality of Satanic power. Nowhere else do we find the presence of evil spirits taken with such seriousness as among these Spirit-filled Christians.

If anyone doubts that our struggle is "against the world rulers of this present darkness, against the spiritual hosts of wickedness in the heavenly places" (Eph. 6:12), let him read Mike Warnke's book, *The Satan-Seller* (Logos, 1973). Mike Warnke was a high priest of Satan, wielding that supernatural power which Satan gives to those who serve him. Mike was delivered from this power, receiving first Jesus Christ and later, the Baptism in the Holy Spirit.

As I look around, I do not see any groups other than the Pentecostals and the charismatics, who understand that each of us is involved in a great cosmic battle between the powers of Satan and Jesus Christ. The people of the Holy Spirit understand this and do not hesitate to exorcise evil spirits in the name of Jesus Christ and by the power of His blood. Thank God we have again discerned the Enemy—Satan!

I realize there are already excesses in the charismatic movement. Some leaders see every form of mental illness, for example, as an evidence of demon possession. On that basis, all that the suicidal person needs, is to have his evil spirit exorcised. But the problem here, it seems to me, is not with the treatment—for some suicidal persons, I am sure, are demon-possessed —but with the diagnosis, or as we would say, the discernment of spirits. The Holy Spirit's gift of discernment (as to whether one is possessed or not), rightly used, will bring us to a more balanced understanding and practice. One of the sanest books I have read on this subject is Michael Harper's *Spiritual Warfare* (Logos, 1970).

As a psychiatric chaplain, I want to add that the understanding of mental illness in terms of a spiritual warfare makes far more sense to me than all these

*Father Schiffmayer in *Newsweek*, June 25, 1973, p. 85b.

psychological theories, the number of which is rapidly becoming legion. The highly questionable theories of Sigmund Freud and the arrogant plans of B. F. Skinner, to cite just two examples, require a faith and trust so great that I must beg off because of my unbelief. It is more than can be asked, I feel, of any man. Lords of humanistic psychology, help thou my unbelief! Accuse me of intellectual and idealistic sloth, but I find myself with faith sufficient only to believe the biblical teaching about God, man, and the devil. The Bible, it seems to me, not only explains the human problem better, but also gives us a proven method to handle the deepest human maladies through spiritual means.

5. *The twentieth-century Pentecost we are experiencing is the more irresistible because it works at making things more simple.* Now, I am sure there are a number of charismatics around whose theological efforts would contradict my statement, but nonetheless, I sense a refreshing tendency toward simplicity in understanding the Christian way and its implications.

It is so easy and tempting to work in the direction of complexity. Egocentrics love to make things intricate and hard to understand. Spirit-filled people work hard at making things simple. That's what Jesus did. He spoke so that children could understand him while the learned became confounded.

Charismatic Christianity, with its emphasis on simplicity, is what my patients basically need and want. One of my patients put it very clearly when he said, "I usually do my thinking in the pit of my stomach. I got no time to read books and attend classes when my depression closes in on me. It takes all the strength I have just to keep my mind fixed on the Lord."

Thank God for Spirit-filled Christians who are trying to keep things simple.

6. *The neo-Pentecostal movement in Christianity is marked also by a new expectation of Christ's imminent return.* This is a needful emphasis in our chaotic

world but no less as a word of hope in the world of the mental hospital.

There is so much in the lives of our hospitalized people which must await a meeting with Jesus Christ before any remedy can be found. Who but Christ can sew up the deep psychic wounds of a schizophrenic? What hope is there for a water-brained alcoholic, other than the hope of Jesus's return? When a retardate finally realizes that he is never going to leave the hospital to live at home with his family, what else can I point him to, other than the present comfort of the Holy Spirit and the future return of Jesus to set things right?

There is hardly a charismatic leader around who does not believe that he will within his lifetime see the return of Jesus.

Proximately, we work for the renewal of broken persons and the social structures in which we live, but ultimately, our hope is in being rescued from this chaotic world-order which is increasingly fit for burning.

I sense so keenly in these last few moments of our fellowship the need for us all to receive and remain open to that Divine Person, the Holy Spirit. "Be filled with the [Holy] Spirit" (Eph. 5:18), says Paul. Let these simple words come true in our hearts.

Holy Spirit: Descend upon us anew and fill every room in our hearts. All our hope is in You. We invite you to work in us and through us into all eternity. In the Name of Jesus. Amen.

We are witnessing a twentieth-century Pentecost.

God is now filling us with His Holy Spirit once again.

The People of the Paraclete are becoming Spirit-empowered, Spirit-disciplined and, most importantly, Spirit-led.

Praise the Lord!

There is nothing more to say.

Praise the Lord!